Facilitating the Development of Women

Nancy J. Evans, *Editor*

NEW DIRECTIONS FOR STUDENT SERVICES
URSULA DELWORTH, GARY R. HANSON, *Editors-in-Chief*

Number 29, March 1985

Paperback sourcebooks in
The Jossey-Bass Higher Education Series

Jossey-Bass Inc., Publishers
San Francisco • Washington • London

Nancy J. Evans (Ed.).
Facilitating the Development of Women.
New Directions for Student Services, no. 29.
San Francisco: Jossey-Bass, 1985.

New Directions for Student Services Series
Ursula Delworth, Gary R. Hanson, *Editors-in-Chief*

New Directions for Student Services (publication number USPS
449-070) is published quarterly by Jossey-Bass Inc., Publishers.
Second-class postage rates paid at San Francisco, California,
and at additional mailing offices.

Correspondence:
Subscriptions, single-issue orders, change of address notices, undelivered
copies, and other correspondence should be sent to Subscriptions,
Jossey-Bass Inc., Publishers, 433 California Street, San Francisco
California 94104.

Editorial correspondence should be sent to the Editors-in-Chief,
Ursula Delworth, University Counseling Service, Iowa
Memorial Union, University of Iowa, Iowa City, Iowa 52242
or Gary R. Hanson, Office of the Dean of Students,
Student Services Building, Room 101, University of Texas
at Austin, Austin, Texas 78712.

Library of Congress Catalogue Card Number LC 84-82378

International Standard Serial Number ISSN 0164-7970

International Standard Book Number ISBN 87589-767-3

Cover art by Willi Baum

Manufactured in the United States of America

Ordering Information

The paperback sourcebooks listed below are published quarterly and can be ordered either by subscription or single-copy.

Subscriptions cost $35.00 per year for institutions, agencies, and libraries. Individuals can subscribe at the special rate of $25.00 per year *if payment is by personal check*. (Note that the full rate of $35.00 applies if payment is by institutional check, even if the subscription is designated for an individual.) Standing orders are accepted. Subscriptions normally begin with the first of the four sourcebooks in the current publication year of the series. When ordering, please indicate if you prefer your subscription to begin with the first issue of the *coming* year.

Single copies are available at $8.95 when payment accompanies order, and *all single-copy orders under $25.00 must include payment*. (California, New Jersey, New York, and Washington, D.C., residents please include appropriate sales tax.) For billed orders, cost per copy is $8.95 plus postage and handling. (Prices subject to change without notice.)

Bulk orders (ten or more copies) of any individual sourcebook are available at the following discounted prices: 10–49 copies, $8.05 each; 50–100 copies, $7.15 each; over 100 copies, *inquire*. Sales tax and postage and handling charges apply as for single copy orders.

To ensure correct and prompt delivery, all orders must give either the *name of an individual* or an *official purchase order number*. Please submit your order as follows:

Subscriptions: specify series and year subscription is to begin.
Single Copies: specify sourcebook code (such as, SS8) and first two words of title.

Mail orders for United States and Possessions, Latin America, Canada, Japan, Australia, and New Zealand to:
Jossey-Bass Inc., Publishers
433 California Street
San Francisco, California 94104

Mail orders for all other parts of the world to:
Jossey-Bass Limited
28 Banner Street
London EC1Y 8QE

New Directions for Student Services Series
Ursula Delworth, Gary R. Hanson, *Editors-in-Chief*

Contents

Editor's Notes

The last decade has seen great increases in the number of women attending institutions of higher education. Today, a slight majority of college students are women (Astin, 1984). Included within this group are increasing numbers of older women and minorities as well as the typical eighteen- to twenty-two-year-olds. The special needs of this diverse group of women students are often overlooked by student affairs professionals who assume that all college students—men and women, young and old, white and nonwhite—have the same needs and react to the college environment similarly. Recent studies of the lives of women demonstrate that important gender differences exist in adult development and that these differences are influenced by changing values concerning the role of women in society (Bardwick, 1980; Gilligan, 1982). This information is important to student affairs practitioners who wish to enhance the development of women on their campuses.

The overall intent of this sourcebook is to advance the knowledge of theory and research related to the development of women and to demonstrate the usefulness of this knowledge in working with young college women, re-entry women, and minority women students. The information provided is intended to encourage professionals in student affairs to develop theoretically sound and creative interventions to address systematically the needs of women students and to ensure that colleges and universities are serving this population adequately, with regard to both academic and personal development. Once differences in development are understood and appreciated, the quality of life for all students will be enhanced.

In Chapter One, Jessie Bernard sets the stage for exploration of women's development by highlighting the significant historical events and changing societal attitudes that have had an impact on the lives of today's college women. She also acknowledges the differing concerns experienced by this diverse group of women.

In Chapter Two, I discuss the development of women across the life span, noting the influence of changing role expectations. I review three schools of thought as they relate to women's development and present recent research findings concerning women's career paths, family roles, interpersonal relationships and self-concept. I suggest ways in which the theoretical concepts and research reviewed can guide student affairs practice with regard to women.

1

Beverly Prosser Gelwick continues the review of recent theory and research in her discussion of the cognitive development of women. In Chapter Three, she explores the impact of Gilligan's work on our understanding of women's development and presents information concerning intellectual development, learning styles, and field dependence-independence as these factors relate to women. Gelwick also discusses implications of this work for students affairs practice.

The next three chapters focus on the specific needs of three subgroups of women and suggest interventions designed to improve our work with them on individual, group, and institutional levels. In Chapter Four, Donna M. Bourassa, Cynthia Woolbright, and I discuss the developmental tasks facing young college women in the areas of career decision making, interpersonal relationships, self-concept, and life-style exploration. We suggest programming needs in these areas and note the roles that student services staff must play in order to encourage the development of this group of women students.

Gay Holliday looks at the experiences and needs of re-entry women in Chapter Five. She identifies barriers to the success of these students and offers specific suggestions for overcoming these barriers.

The history of minorities in this country and the unique needs and issues experienced by black, native American, Hispanic, and Asian-American women are not topics generally presented in student affairs preparation programs. In Chapter Six, Carolyn R. Payton provides information about these groups and advocates increased recruitment efforts, more financial aid, and programming to address the concerns of these students.

Addressing the concerns of women students requires administrative support. In Chapter Seven, Susan R. Komives and I point out some of the barriers facing those of us who wish to present a coherent proactive program to meet the developmental needs of women students. We then suggest an action agenda designed to improve the quality of the college experience for women students. We also advocate the application of feminist principles to student affairs divisions. The chapter concludes with some specific suggestions for future research to explore further women's development, the effect of programs for women, and the impact of college on women.

Finally, in Chapter Eight, Cathleen M. Barrett and I present a fairly representative sample of literature discussing women's development and programming for women. These books and articles should be useful to student affairs practitioners who wish to explore these topics further.

Nancy J. Evans
Editor

References

Astin, A. W. "A Look at Pluralism in the Contemporary Student Population." *NASPA Journal*, 1984, *21* (3), 2-12.

Bardwick, J. M. "The Seasons of a Woman's Life." In D. G. McGuigan (Ed.), *Women's Lives: New Theory, Research, and Policy.* Ann Arbor: University of Michigan, Center for Continuing Education of Women, 1980.

Gilligan, C. *In a Different Voice: Psychological Theory and Women's Development.* Cambridge, Mass.: Harvard University Press, 1982.

Nancy J. Evans is assistant professor of higher education and student affairs at Indiana University. She has held positions in residence life, student activities, and counseling at several colleges and universities.

Today's college women live in a society in which expectations and opportunities for women are changing rapidly.

Introduction: College Women in a Changing Society

Jessie Bernard

It is a mark of our times that books like this one are called for, to update our rapidly expanding knowledge about human development and to incorporate this knowledge into our services to—in this case—women students. The impact of societal change on women has to be constantly monitored if we wish to keep our services to women students current. The cohorts of young women who will be undergraduates in the last fifteen years of this millenium will have been born in the mid 1960s or later; their experiences will have been much different than those of the faculty and student affairs professionals who will be attempting to meet their needs.

These young women will not have lived through the anguish and excitement of the early days of the civil rights movement; they will not remember the activism and turmoil of the Vietnam War era; the assassinations of the Kennedys and Martin Luther King will be merely events they read about in history class. They will have been children during the crisis in marriage that occurred between the mid 1960s and mid 1970s—a decade in which marriage declined, divorce more than doubled, and cohabitation increased significantly (Bernard, 1982). The

N. J. Evans (Ed.). *Facilitating the Development of Women.* New Directions for Student Services, no. 29. San Francisco: Jossey-Bass, March 1985.

older of them may remember when their mothers decided to enter the labor force, since 1980 marked a "tipping point" when more than half of mothers with children under eighteen were in the work force. Indeed, they will be among the first cohort of children who will really show the impact of that momentous decision of mothers to work outside the home. All of these young college women will have been affected to some extent by the economic recession of the late 1970s and early 1980s. As Levine (1980) points out, these historical conditions have influenced the expectations and values of today's college students, leading to conservatism, materialism, and a focus on self.

College women are also experiencing the benefits of the early successes of the feminist movement. Sex roles are becoming more flexible while attitudes toward acceptable life-styles for women are more enlightened. If women students "want it all," there are plenty of models around them. They will not consider it unusual that women are being taken seriously, as Supreme Court justices or as candidates for the vice-presidency.

Unfortunately, today's college women are also being bombarded with proof that the ambitions of college women of the 1970s have harvested a bitter fruit, that success has meant disillusionment, and that career achievement has meant failure in interpersonal relationships. The undergraduate woman still sees women depicted in popular culture as dumb blondes or predatory brunettes, images that in no way correspond with her view of herself. There are subtle but constant negative presentations of feminism as man-hating and of "women's libbers" as not quite "with it." These mixed messages, ambiguous statements, and conflicting expectations create stress and uncertainty in the lives of college women. Student services professionals must be sensitive to the effects of societal conditions and assist students in clarifying their values and decision making in the face of often unclear expectations.

Those engaged in serving college women may take it for granted that students will be receiving good information about the most recent research on sex differences. But this research will tend to have a male bias that often has the effect, if not the intent, of judging women by male-defined criteria and finding them not quite up to standard (Broverman and others, 1972). As a result, some women have become "minimalistic" with respect to sex differences, downplaying them as much as possible. But the growing critique of the male-biased research (Gilligan, 1982; Horner, 1971) is helping women to overcome the negative self-image fostered by it and to gain recognition of the great strengths of women (Miller, 1976).

Unfortunately, sociology has been slower than psychology to investigate the experiences of women. Although college women have the opportunity to learn a significant amount about individual sex differences in development, they will probably have relatively little chance to explore differences between the male and female worlds. As with psychological differences, so also differences in male and female social environments have been delineated from a male point of view. The male world has been the standard; the female world has been considered generally inferior. As research findings accumulate about the female world, women feel less apologetic about it. They no longer believe that it must change to conform to the male model. Especially significant is the recent research on the importance of friendship in the lives of women (Smith-Rosenberg, 1975) and the role played by support groups, both in family life and careers. Student services professionals have an obligation to familiarize themselves with the new scholarship on women, to pass this information on to their students, and to incorporate it into a better-designed system of services to women on their campuses.

College women today are a diverse group confronting a wide range of developmental issues. Young undergraduate women face the task of choosing among a variety of life options. The idea of deliberately scheduling the major events in life — marriage, timing and spacing of children, timing of professional training, timing of one's first job — is becoming expected. Long-range planning is not something women have traditionally been involved in. The result is often stress and difficulty in decision making. Student affairs practitioners must recognize the pressures that accompany increased options.

The women returning to school during the final fifteen years of the century will find a student body and faculty more accustomed to their presence than did the pioneers who re-entered college during earlier decades. They will be educationally less disadvantaged than those earlier returning women students, but they will still find college policies and procedures that demonstrate an insensitivity to their needs. These new returning women students will require concerned and knowledgeable student affairs staff to help them overcome the barriers and address the life changes involved in their decision to return to college.

The diversity of minority students means that, although they all share some similar needs, each group also has unique concerns. When compared with black students in earlier decades, today's black undergraduate women have more career opportunities available to them as well as greater numbers of achieving women — great writers, poets, artists, scientists, and political leaders — to serve as models. But they are still vulnerable to the two-way oppression of both sexism and racism. Asian-American women appear on the surface to be outstanding achievers, yet they experience significant developmental issues related to interpersonal relationships and self-concept. The differences among Hispanic women mean that undergraduates in Florida will have one set of needs; those in Texas or California, another; and those in New York or Chicago, still another. And the issues facing native American college women are complicated by the decisions they must make concerning the extent to which they will accommodate to the prevailing American culture.

In light of the diversity found among women attending college today, those in the profession of serving students need to continue to be anthropologists, sociologists, and psychologists as well as educators. This book can speed them along the way.

References

Bernard, J. *The Future of Marriage.* New Haven, Conn.: Yale University Press, 1982.

Broverman, I. K., Vogel, S. R., Broverman, D. M., Clarkson, F. E., and Rosenkrantz, P. S. "Sex-Role Stereotypes: A Current Appraisal." *Journal of Social Issues,* 1972, *28* (2), 59–78.

Gilligan, C. *In a Different Voice: Psychological Theory and Women's Development.* Cambridge, Mass.: Harvard University Press, 1982.

Horner, M. S. "Fail: Bright Women." In A. Theodore (Ed.), *The Professional Woman.* Cambridge, Mass.: Schenkman, 1971.

Levine, A. *When Dreams and Heroes Died: A Portrait of Today's College Student.* San Francisco: Jossey-Bass, 1980.

Miller, J. B. *Toward a New Psychology of Women.* Boston: Beacon Press, 1976.

Smith-Rosenberg, C. "The Female World of Love and Ritual: Relations Between Women in Nineteenth-Century America." *Signs,* 1975, *1* (1), 1–29.

Jessie Bernard is professor emerita at Pennsylvania State University. She is past vice-president of the American Sociological Association, which has named an award in her honor.

In a time of rapidly changing societal norms and role expectations, the lives of women are becoming increasingly complex and varied.

Women's Development Across the Life Span

Nancy J. Evans

Investigation of developmental change across the life span is a recent phenomenon. Only in the last three decades has this topic appeared in the psychological literature. Largely as a result of the psychoanalytic influence, development was thought to end once a person reached adolescence. Adults then settled into life with their basic personality developed, valued intact, and decisions made (George, 1982; Schlossberg, 1984).

Erikson (1968) was one of the first major theorists to suggest that growth and change during the adult years were normal and necessary processes. Like most of the theorists who followed him, Erikson dealt with the male life cycle. Women's development, if mentioned at all, was viewed in a very narrow way and often judged as abnormal for not adhering to the male pattern. Erikson (1968) did not believe that a women's identity was formed until after marriage. As late as 1963, Mulvey wrote that, for women, "the married state, unbroken and continuous, irrespective of family and/or employment status, is the greatest single contributor to the highest level of adjustment, and thus is a necessary element for a mature integration of personality" (p. 380). As

N. J. Evans (Ed.). *Facilitating the Development of Women.* New Directions for Student Services, no. 29. San Francisco: Jossey-Bass, March 1985.

Bernard (1981) points out, theorists reduced the lives of women to stages in their reproductive cycle or equated women's development with the family life cycle (Coup and others, 1973; Glick, 1957; Lopata, 1971).

Giele (1982a) suggests that the image that people have of women as wives and mothers has led to an underestimation of the importance of other aspects of their lives. The failure of theorists to explore the increasingly central role of work in the lives of women is particularly problematic. Major theories of adult development also fail to consider the possibility that women may view their world differently than men and establish their value systems based on those differences. Women appear to be more sensitive to other people, for example, and to respond more significantly to loss (Gilligan, 1982; Miller, 1976).

Giele (1982b) saw two trends influencing the recognition and acceptance of sex differences in the adult life cycle: (a) a willingness to explore different themes in the lives of women and (b) an increased sense of changes in women's roles over the course of time. This chapter will discuss the development of women across the life span, taking into account both of these trends. Because of the overriding influence societal change has had on the lives of women, this topic will be the first considered. The varied and conflicting role expectations facing modern women will be discussed in light of these historical changes. Next, three major theoretical approaches to adult development will be presented, and their relevance to the study of women's lives will also be considered. The chapter will close with a discussion of the utility for student affairs practice of the theory and research reviewed here.

Societal Change and Changing Role Expectations

Historical change in society can have a profound effect on women's lives. The life experience of women of a particular age may result in a distinctive developmental pattern not found among older or younger women (Giele, 1982b). Perun (1981) went so far as to suggest that stress and crisis found in the lives of middle-aged women could be assumed to be related to societal change rather than to psychological factors until proved otherwise.

Certainly, the changes that have occurred in society over the last two centuries are extensive. Life course transitions have become more strictly age related and more individually oriented rather than influenced by family needs (Hareven, 1980). Looking at more recent social change, Giele (1982a) has noted the focus on family life and material comfort following World War II. Fairly rigid sex roles were the norm. Since 1950, however, societal changes have mitigated against this clear separation of roles. The birthrate has declined, people are postponing marriage, women are living longer, divorce is more likely, and more time is available after children leave home (Giele, 1982b). Increasing numbers of women are now in the work force. In 1980, 52 percent of all women over sixteen years of age were working, and 45 percent of mothers with preschool-age children were employed (Waite, 1981).

The result of these changes has been an increase in the options available to women. The mix of family and work roles is much greater than it has been in the past and much more extensive than the options available to men. Tasks once thought to be exclusively the purview of men are now increasingly being performed by women (Giele, 1982b).

The rapid historical change witnessed over the last decades has resulted in changing, varied, and often contradictory role expectations for women. Surveys regarding the role of women in society all report movement toward more egalitarian attitudes, particularly among the young, the educated, and those with women workers in their families (Giele, 1982b). Greater acceptance of women's employment outside the home is particularly noteworthy (Giele, 1982c). Programs and policies including affimative action, flexible working hours, childcare services, and pension coverage for women constitute visible support of working women (Giele, 1982b). In fact, Bernard (1975) argues that it is the housewives who must defend their role rather than women who are employed outside the home. The increase in the number of women in the labor force has also led to greater sharing of household and parenting tasks (Kanter, 1977).

While these new patterns demonstrate less separation of work and family roles, men still appear to have more responsibility for wage earning and women for care giving and household maintenance (Giele, 1982c). Modern couples still tend to make decisions concerning geographical location and timing of major family events based on the husband's career needs (Giele, 1982c).

For many women, traditional sex-role expectations are still salient, especially in adolescence and early adulthood (Bardwick, 1980). Young women still see their future in terms of marriage, ignoring the statistics concerning divorce, years of childlessness, and mortality rates for men over fifty (Bardwick, 1980; Giele, 1982c). Strommer (1976) reported that 9 percent of American women see marriage as "the best way to live" (p. 84). Apparently women still accept stereotypes that women cannot develop their fullest potential if they do not marry and raise children.

A prevailing norm in society, even for those who have moved beyond traditional roles, is that femininity is equated with passivity, dependency, and pleasing men (Bernard, 1975). Both in their marital roles and in their work roles, women are expected to assume helping and nurturing roles and to follow the lead of men (Wells and Loring, 1978).

The conflicting choices and norms facing women result in ambiguity and personal uncertainty. Strains experienced by the individual are greater because of the lack of clear societal guidelines and support. Modern women face significant challenges in negotiating the life course to "have it all."

Theoretical Perspectives

Increasing interest within the disciplines of psychology and sociology has led to the construction of a number of models of adult development. Each model presents a general orientation to this topic, assisting in interpretation of behavior and guiding researchers in their investigations of change over the life span. Models of adult development can be grouped on the basis of four assumptions: (a) the degree to which predictability or variability throughout the life course is emphasized, (b) whether development is linked to chronological age, (c) whether change is assumed to originate within the person or the environment, and (d) the degree to which change is viewed as a crisis (George, 1982; Schlossberg, 1984). Three models of adult development will be reviewed: life stage, life events, and individual timing perspectives.

Life Stage Perspectives. The life stage perspectives have their origin in psychology and as such tend to focus on the individual, emphasizing personality, cognition, and other intrapsychic factors. According to these theorists, change is initiated by an internal timetable that is influenced only in a minor way be environmental events. Adults become more individuated and complex throughout their lives, with later developmental tasks building on earlier ones in a predictable progression. Failure to complete successfully a developmental task is viewed as seriously inhibiting development later in life. Life stage perspectives differ according to the degree to which they see developmental tasks as (a) age linked, (b) specific rather than general, and (c) characterized by continuity versus discontinuity (Giele, 1982b; George, 1982; Rossi, 1980). Theorists falling within the life stage perspective include Erikson (1968), Levinson (1978), and Gould (1978).

The life stage perspectives are based almost exclusively on the male experience and may not make sense for women. Several writers have attempted to modify Levinson's model of adult development to fit the life experience of women (Chickering and Havighurst, 1981; Lehmann, 1978; Sales, 1978). Others have tried to develop stage models that fit the lives of women more closely (Scarf, 1980). An examination of these attempts suggests that the varied experiences of women are hard to categorize as occurring at specific ages or in sequential stages. Research bears out this observation.

In a study examining the age-thirty transition (one of Levinson's stages) for women, Stewart (1977) found that women experience greater variation in the order in which they accomplish specific tasks and in the degree of difficulty they have in establishing a satisfactory life structure. In another study (Barnett and Baruch, 1980) the only one of Levinson's (1978) four developmental tasks of early adulthood that had meaning in the lives of young women was "forming a love attachment." Unlike men in Levinson's study, women in this study seldom had mentors and were rarely in a position to reassess commitments by age forty since many did not enter the work world until their thirties. Other researchers have been unable to identify age-related stages in women's development (Notman, 1979; Rubin, 1979; Sangiuliano, 1980) or the existence of a midlife crisis (Serlin, 1980). Life stage development seems most similar for the sexes early and late in life. The timing and ordering of family and career cycles for women show much greater diversity than for men, requiring more balancing and integrating of roles.

Life Events Perspectives. The life events perspectives acknowledge the important role of timing, duration, spacing, and ordering of life events on human development. Developmental events are not necessarily linked to specific ages. Life events are defined as "identifiable discrete changes in usual patterns of behavior, changes that can create stress and can pose adaptive challenges to the individual" (George, 1982, p. 27). Thus, the focus is on environmental influences leading to behavioral change and the intertwining of many different dimensions of development over the life span (Giele, 1982b; Rossi, 1980). Among the theorists within the life events perspective are Fiske (formerly Lowenthal) (1980), Perun and Bielby (1980), George (1980), Pearlin (1980), and Schlossberg (1984).

The focus on variability and environmental factors makes this perspective particularly applicable to women's lives. Perun and Bielby (1980) suggest, in fact, that changes in women's lives present the best evidence of the existence and consequences of variability in the life course structure. They conducted a study of academic women social scientists that identified three patterns of family and work cycles. The age at which various life events occurred varied widely according to the pattern chosen and showed greater consistency within each pattern. No one pattern led to greater achievement than another.

Manis (1980) also identified a wide variety of patterns in the lives of women who made a transition from homemaker to employment. She found that the order in which they finished college, married, worked, stayed home, went to graduate school, and returned to work varied considerably.

Other studies of work and family histories of women show a great many combinations of developmental tasks and life events and suggest that no one pattern is most successful (Best, 1978; Daniels and Weingarten, 1982).

Individual Timing Perspectives. Those who view adult development from an individual timing perspective stress the variability of adult life and downplay the role of biology in human growth and change. They point out that two ten-year-olds are a great deal more similar than two sixty-year-olds because of the "individual fanning-out process" (Neugarten, 1976). Environmental influences affect human development in a number of ways. First, everyone develops a "social clock" that indicates what behaviors are appropriate at particular ages. Social time is influenced by historical time; the expectations concerning age-appropriate behavior have varied over time. Stress occurs when people experience events that are "off-time" or unexpected (Neugarten, 1976; Rossi, 1980; Schlossberg, 1984). Neugarten (1976) and Vaillant (1977) are the major proponents of the individual timing perspective.

Several studies indicate that the individual timing perspective can be used to describe the lives of women. Wiersma (1980) determined that, in a sample of traditional women, midlife was identified more by events on the social clock, such as children leaving home, the death of parents, and career plateaus, than by chronological age. Both Neugarten (1976) and Targ (1979) found that nonnormal, unanticipated events, such as divorce or widowhood at a young age, are much more traumatic than events such as menopause, which are expected.

Dimensions of the Life Course

The lives of women are made up of a number of intertwining dimensions that vary in importance over the life course and that greatly influence each other. The family life cycle, career paths, interpersonal relationships, and self-concept and sense of well-being will be considered separately and then discussed as interconnected facets of a women's life.

Family Roles. Societal expectations concerning the family life cycle are still fairly rigid, especially for women: They are expected to marry and have children and to subsume their career pursuits to the needs and desires of their husband and family. In spite of these attitudes, women's decisions concerning family roles are changing. They are postponing marriage, having fewer children and having them later in life, experiencing divorce and widowhood more frequently, and often combining work and family roles (Kitagawa, 1981; Van Dusen and Sheldon, 1976). This section will review the various family roles assumed by women and explore the effects of family life-style on women's lives.

Women often have a more difficult time separating from their family of origin and are more influenced by the expectations of their parents than men (Menaker, 1979). They are usually expected to maintain closer contact with their families and to care for them when necessary (Arcana, 1979; Rubin, 1976).

More than nine out of ten women over the age of 35 have been married at least once, and most of these women have had at least one child (O'Rand and Henretta, 1982). The timing of these events varies considerably and many women are now combining these roles with full- or part-time employment outside the home. Women who do not work tend to marry earlier, to have their children before the age of thirty, to have their first child within the first four years of their marriage, and to have more than two children. Professional women, on the other hand, tend to have smaller families, to wait longer after marriage to have children, and to have their children at a relatively late age. They report that their career did influence the size of their family and the timing and spacing of their children (Holmstrom, 1978). Women in professional careers are likely to have fewer children than their male counterparts (Giele, 1982c) and to experience guilt feelings concerning their children's care (Menaker, 1979). Despite the willingness of men to be more involved in child and household care (Giele, 1982c), responsibility for these tasks still falls primarily to women, whether they work outside the home or not (Hedges, 1978).

The age at which women bear children affects their life course significantly. Those who have their first child before their twentieth birthday or before or during their first year of marriage are more likely to experience divorce, to obtain less education, to work less and in lower-paying jobs, and to become dependent on welfare (Moore and others, 1980). On the other hand, women who bear children later in life seem to have more difficulties with childrearing (Rossi, 1980). Those women who have large families also found raising children more difficult, perhaps because of financial pressures.

Studies examining the satisfaction of women with the parenting role have produced conflicting results. A U-shaped pattern of marital satisfaction has been found, indicating that the childrearing years produce the greatest amount of stress for women (Rollins and Galligan, 1978), yet Serlin (1980) reported that children were a major source of happiness for women in all stages of their lives.

Serlin (1980) found that family roles, even for women who worked full-time, were more important in the lives of women than were the work roles. While additional role expectations are increasing the stress felt by many mothers with children, their anxieties seem to be offset by the rewards this role brings.

In spite of strong social pressure to have children, increasing numbers of women are choosing to remain childless. Childless married women report a variety of reasons for their decision: unhappy childhood and family experiences, a dislike of children, a desire to preserve the quality of their married relationship, and fear of reverting to traditional sex roles. For many, career was a major consideration (Fabe and Wikler, 1979). While childless wives experience some regret about their decision, they feel that they are adequately compensated by other satisfactions and interests (Holmstrom, 1978).

The divorce rates have doubled since 1965; 37 per 1,000 marriages now end in divorce (Kitagawa, 1981). Among professional women the divorce rate is even higher (Strommer, 1976). The increasing frequency of divorce has resulted in a large increase in one-parent families; 90 percent of these are maintained by the mother (Kitagawa, 1981). Divorced women, especially those who have been full-time homemakers, often have a difficult time becoming economically self-sufficient and regaining a sense of self-worth and emotional independence (Targ, 1979).

In 1979, 20 percent of all women twenty-five to twenty-nine were single (Kitagawa, 1981). Among career women, marriage rates are often quite low. Studies indicate that 50 percent of successful business women and 45 percent of women holding doctorates are unmarried (Holmstrom, 1978). Single professional women tend to center their lives around their careers and lack support for development in other areas of their lives. Age thirty is often a time of crisis as single women reach early goals and reevaluate what they want from life (Evans and others, 1981; Kangas, 1976). Single women experience more stress than married women and are less likely to report being happy, especially as they age (Antonucci and others, 1980; Cargan and Melko, 1982).

Career Decisions and Career Paths. The career paths of women are becoming more similar to men's, with more women working during young adulthood and exhibiting continuous work patterns (Giele, 1982c). Between 1950 and 1973, the number of women working rose by one-third, with the greatest increase being among women between twenty-five and thirty-four years of age (Van Dusen and Sheldon, 1976). Masnick and Bane (1980) noted three revolutions in women's work: (a) a revolution in rate of participation, (b) an increase in women's commitment to work, and (c) a revolution in women's contribution to family income. They suggested that the first revolution is completed, the second underway, and the third is yet to come.

In spite of the increased rate of participation of women in the labor force, no formal theory of women's career development exists. Perun and Bielby (1981) critiqued existing theories of career development and pointed out that they either lack a life course focus, fail to include women in their validation samples, or lack comprehensiveness. Young (1978) discusses various combinations of women's work and family patterns, coming up with eight possible role sequences. Corcoran (1978) presents a schema of work patterns that eliminates the connection to the family life cycle. She found that a continuous work pattern was the most common among women she studied.

A number of researchers have attempted to identify factors in a woman's background that shape her orientation toward work. Family relationships have been linked to women's career decisions. Career women are more likely to have had working mothers (Radloff and Monroe, 1978), close relationships with their fathers (Kahn, 1979), more freedom (Elder, 1974), and rewards for assertiveness (Kahn, 1979).

Ginzberg (1966) suggested that women cannot realistically plan a career until they know what kind of man they will marry and that greater uncertainty in planning is a major difference between men and women in career development. Unfortunately, Barnett and Baruch (1980) found research evidence to support his claim. Women interviewed between the ages of thirty-five and fifty-five, in recalling their motivations at ages sixteen to seventeen, indicated that they never thought about how their economic needs would be met. Although they expected to work, they did not see work as a long-term commitment. Most anticipated "Prince Charming" to show up and take care of them. Hennig and Jardim (1977) found that, for most women, career decisions are passive, made when they realize they are probably going to work for the rest of their lives. Women tend to attribute any career success to luck or the support of a supervisor.

Work can have positive effects on women's lives. In a sample of gifted women surveyed in their sixties, those who had worked most of their lives were more satisfied than those who had been homemakers. They also felt that they had more control over their lives (Willemsen, 1980). A sense of autonomy and competence was also reported by working mothers of preschool children (Plunkett, 1980). Some practical outcomes of working were identified as social contact with other adults, less dependence on husbands, and being able to contribute more to discussions (Plunkett, 1980). Markus (1980) points out that the relationship between work and a woman's sense of well-being is contingent on the woman's view of herself and her role in life. Working is a positive experience for those who see themselves as career women or who see benefits to be gained from employment.

Uninterrupted educational and career involvement seem to be required for outstanding career achievement (Chickering and Havighurst, 1981). Bernard (1981) believes that a pattern that involves childrearing between professional training and beginning a career will handicap a woman in establishing herself professionally. Successful career women often marry later and seldom have children or have them later in life (O'Rand and Henretta, 1982). Childrearing, generally, is viewed as being a much more powerful inhibitor of career success than is marriage (Bernard, 1981).

Despite the potential career problems attached to dropping out of the work force during the young adult years, many women do not work during this time if they have preschool children. Faver (1980) suggests that external constraints rather than psychological factors lead to this decision in many cases. Women experience problems getting help from their husbands and others with household and childrearing tasks; in securing part-time employment, necessary absences, and adequate transportation; and in combatting their husbands' negative attitudes about their working. Professional women have been found to limit their career ambitions to maintain harmony in their families (Hedges, 1978).

Delayed career entry also entails certain problems. Many professions, including business and medicine, do not welcome older individuals into training programs or professional schools (Chickering and Havighurst, 1981). Women beginning careers after children are grown may not be able to accumulate experience that leads to greater occupational opportunities and financial rewards (O'Rand and Henretta, 1982). Given the present structure of the work world, perhaps we do women entering the labor force later in life a disservice by suggesting that significant career opportunities await them.

Interpersonal Relationships. Relationships outside marriage seem to play a more significant role in women's lives than they do for men. Compared to men, women have more friends and form more intimate and reciprocal relationships (Lowenthal and others, 1975). Women are also more affected by events in the lives of those close to them, perhaps because they have devoted more effort to the relationships (Rossi, 1980).

Friendship patterns change over time for women. Women at midlife seem to have less time and energy to give to the formation of friendships than do older women (Block and others, 1981). Preretirement women tend to have more friends and are able to provide more complex descriptions of their friends than are younger women (Lowenthal and others, 1975).

Friendships are particularly important to single women who look to friends for nurturance and support (Kangas, 1976). Single women, however, are often perceived as competition by married women and may be limited by their professional status in finding friends with the same interests.

Friends and other support systems serve as a buffer against stress for women (Barnett and Baruch, 1978). Women frequently call on friends to assist them in facing transitions and role losses such as divorce, widowhood, and retirement and in managing increasingly complicated lives (Robertson, 1978).

Self-Concept and Well-Being. Differences in self-concept and sense of well-being between men and women are reported in the literature. A consistent theme is women's tendency to define themselves in terms of their relationships to others (Gilligan, 1982; Miller, 1976; Notman, 1979; Scarf, 1980). While maturity in men is viewed as a process of developing autonomy, for women it is meeting responsibilities within relationships (Bardwick, 1980; Gilligan, 1982).

Men have been found to possess a more positive self-image than women, particularly prior to midlife (Lowenthal and others, 1975). Women feel a lack of control in their lives (Lowenthal and others, 1975), worry more, and are more willing to admit shortcomings than men (Antonucci and others, 1980). Women are also more adaptable than men (Sales, 1978), have a greater tolerance for ambiguity, and have richer and more complex affective lives (Lowenthal and others, 1975).

Midlife seems to be a particularly hard time for women. Women are more pessimistic and conflicted during this period than they are at other stages (Lowenthal and others, 1975). Once past this period, however, women turn outward, become more assertive, increase in aspiration level, and see themselves as more resourceful, independent, persistent, and idealistic (Lehmann, 1978; Lowenthal and others, 1975).

Psychological disturbance, especially depression, occurs with greater frequency among women than among men (Weissman and Klerman, 1977). Learned or real helplessness, often associated with the passive, isolated, emotionally dependent role women have traditionally been expected to play, has been linked to depression (Radloff and Monroe, 1978). Women particularly vulnerable to physical and psychological disturbances are those who have significant caretaking responsibilities and a lack of support: heads of single-parent families and married women with small children (Gove and Hughes, 1979).

In general, women who have a high sense of competence and self-esteem also experience a sense of well-being (Miller, 1976). Competence and self-esteem are linked both to the structure of the roles in which a woman finds herself and to the values attached to those roles, both by the woman herself and by society (Barnett and Baruch, 1978; Giele, 1982b).

The Intertwining of the Dimensions of a Woman's Life. The literature reviewed highlights the extent to which the various roles assumed by women are interrelated. Women's development has been described as a "braid of threads in which colors appear, disappear, and reappear" (McGuigan, 1980, p. xii). A decision to have a child may mean postponing one's career entry, which might lead to a sense of dissatisfaction and lack of fulfillment. The lack of an adequate friendship network may make an unanticipated divorce particularly difficult, causing depression and lowering a woman's self-esteem. The decision to enter a demanding profession may result in a postponement of marriage and the inability to find friends with similar interests. The combinations are endless.

Men and women differ in the degree to which they perceive the roles in their lives as interconnected. For men, occupation is viewed as separate from marriage and parenthood, while, for women, the three roles are linked (Tittle, 1982). Decisions women make in one area of their lives greatly affect, and are affected by, decisions in other areas. As a result, planning becomes more difficult, women's lives are more complex and less predictable, and the stress experienced by women is often great. As student affairs professionals, we have an obligation to inform and support our women students as they confront the decisions in their lives.

Implications for Student Affairs Practice

Theory and research must be translated into practical ideas to be useful. In this chapter an enormous amount of material has been reviewed. This section will provide some general suggestions for using these theoretical propositions and data to guide our work with individual women students, to undergird programming, and to determine institutional policy. These ideas will be expanded in later chapters of this sourcebook.

Working with Women Students Individually. The data on societal change and changing role expectations tell us that women students on our campuses will be varied. An increasing number of eighteen- to twenty-two-year-old women are enrolling in college. Along with this age group, other women, from twenty-two to over seventy, are entering or returning to school. As we have seen, the life circumstances, motivations, and needs of these women vary greatly.

Young women today are experiencing a different life than that which faced most student affairs professionals as they entered adulthood. The norms are more varied and the role expectations, while more open, are often confusing. As Komives and I note in Chapter Seven, student services personnel, both men and women, must be sensitive to these differences and refrain from imposing their values on the young women with whom they work. They have an obligation, however, to assist women in exploring and clarifying their values within the context of an often contradictory society.

A major responsibility of student affairs professionals is to inform students of their options and the consequences of various options they might choose. Data suggest that women are poor planners (Barnett and Baruch, 1980). Knowledge of possible career opportunities, life-style possibilities, and the trade-offs of various combinations of roles can be beneficial in breaking this pattern. Individual counseling and career development interventions for young women are presented in Chapter Four.

In Chapter Seven, Komives and I emphasize the importance of encouraging women to assume leadership roles on campus. Experience making meaningful decisions, handling crises, and mediating interpersonal conflicts provides women with the confidence and skills necessary to handle themselves assertively in professional work settings and to maintain their identity within marriage and interpersonal relationships. Self-esteem and a sense of well-being are built on successful experiences when women feel in control of their lives.

While the primary task for student affairs professionals in working with younger women students is to inform and support decision making while building self-esteem, their role in working with older women is to assist them in adapting to transition in their lives. For many women, returning to school means adding one more role to a list that already includes wife, mother, friend, and community volunteer.

Such women may need assistance in learning how to keep all the balls in the air at the same time. For other women, returning to school closely follows a loss — divorce, widowhood, or children leaving home. In such cases, women may be experiencing a loss of self-esteem, grief, or depression in addition to anxiety about making it in the academic world. In Chapter Five, Holliday discusses the importance of providing counseling and supportive listeners for women facing such situations.

Older women need accurate information concerning career options. Discrimination against older individuals entering the work force must be discussed, and realistic strategies for combatting it need to be presented. When possible, older women should be encouraged to obtain practical work experience via internships and part-time employment and to emphasize the skills they have gained through volunteer activities.

Programming. Women's strong relational orientation provides a solid rationale for the use of group experiences to facilitate development. Women are influenced by others and receive support and encouragement from them. These traits can be of benefit as women consider decisions and confront transitions in their lives.

Life planning and career decision making are crucial topics for young women living in a society where values and expectations are changing rapidly. These are excellent issues to address in small groups or workshops where individuals can share ideas and be challenged and supported by their peers. Addressing the important decisions in one's life becomes a bit less scary among others who are in the same position. In Chapter Four, Bourassa, Woolbright, and I suggest a number of group strategies for life planning, career decision making, and self-exploration. We also advocate the use of role models and mentors in programming for women.

For older women, support groups are crucial as they face the transition of becoming a student. Meeting and developing friendships with other women in the same situation help offset the feeling of being different and "off-time." In Chapter Five, Holliday offers several ideas for using support groups and workshops to explore topics important in the lives of returning women students. Such programs can help women develop coping skills, including strategies for adapting to a new life-style.

Institutional Policy. If colleges and universities are to support and encourage the development of women students, they need to begin by reexamining the image they present and the mission they endorse. Our educational system is male dominated and male oriented in its structure. To a large extent, men hold top-level positions and women are assistant professors, secretaries, and custodial staff. The image portrayed to women students is that women can work, but only in lesser positions under the supervision of men. Women role models in the highest positions on campus are important if we are to combat this pervasive attitude.

The competitive, lock-step male employment pattern is also held up to our students as the only way to "make it." This attitude is apparent in the failure of women who try alternative paths to gain tenure as well as in the messages faculty give women students interested in careers. Colleges must become more visibly open to part-time employment of faculty and staff, to job sharing, and to extended leaves, patterns that demonstrate a value system more conducive to the needs of women.

Colleges must be sensitive to the needs of older women students who are often attending school while maintaining a variety of other roles. In Chapter Five, Holliday addresses the special concerns of re-entry women with regard to scheduling, financial aid, recruitment, and other areas needing institutional awareness and support.

The developmental tasks and life events facing women today are changing, varied, and complex. As Komives and I stress in Chapter Seven, faculty, administrators, and staff must be made aware of the concerns of today's women students. In addition to meeting the needs of women students directly, student affairs staff must take the lead in seeing that the knowledge and sensitivity of their colleagues is increased.

References

Antonucci, T., Tamir, L. M., and Dubnoff, S. "Mental Health Across the Family Life Cycle." In K. W. Back (Ed.), *Life Course: Integrative Theories and Exemplary Populations.* Boulder, Colo.: Westview Press, 1980.

Arcana, J. *Our Mother's Daughters.* Berkeley: Shameless Hussy Press, 1979.

Bardwick, J. M. "The Seasons of a Woman's Life." In D. G. McGuigan (Ed.), *Women's Lives: New Theory, Research, and Policy.* Ann Arbor: University of Michigan, Center for Continuing Education of Women, 1980.

Barnett, R. C., and Baruch, G. K. "Women in the Middle Years: A Critique of Research and Theory." *Psychology of Women Quarterly,* 1978, *3* (2), 187–197.

Barnett, R. C., and Baruch, G. K. "Toward Economic Independence: Women's Involvement in Multiple Roles." In D. G. McGuigan (Ed.), *Women's Lives: New Theory, Research, and Policy.* Ann Arbor: University of Michigan, Center for Continuing Education of Women, 1980.

Bernard, J. *Women, Wives, Mothers: Values and Options.* Hawthorne, N. Y.: Aldine, 1975.

Bernard, J. "Women's Educational Needs." In A. W. Chickering and Associates (Eds.), *The Modern American College: Responding to the New Realities of Diverse Students and a Changing Society.* San Francisco: Jossey-Bass, 1981.

Best, F. "The Time of Our Lives: The Parameters of Work-Life Scheduling." *Society and Leisure,* 1978, *1* (1), 95–124.

Block, M. R., Davidson, J. L., and Grambs, J. D. *Women Over Forty: Visions and Realities.* New York: Springer, 1981.

Cargan, L., and Melko, M. *Singles: Myths and Realities.* Beverly Hills, Calif.: Sage, 1982.

Chickering, A. W., and Havighurst, R. D. "The Life Cycle." In A. W. Chickering and Associates (Eds.), *The Modern American College: Responding to the New Realities of Diverse Students and a Changing Society.* San Francisco: Jossey-Bass, 1981.

Corcoran, M. "Work Experience, Work Interruption, and Wages." In G. J. Duncan and J. N. Morgan (Eds.), *Five Thousand American Families — Patterns of Economic Progress.* Ann Arbor: University of Michigan, Institute for Social Research, 1978.

Coup, R. F., Greene, S., and Gardner, B. B. *A Study of Working-Class Women in a Changing World.* Chicago: Social Research, 1973.

Daniels, P., and Weingarten, K. *Sooner or Later: The Timing of Parenthood in Adult Lives.* New York: Norton, 1982.

Elder, G. H., Jr. *Children of the Great Depression: Social Change in Life Experience.* Chicago: University of Chicago Press, 1974.

Erikson, E. H. *Identity: Youth and Crisis.* New York: Norton, 1968.

Evans, N. J., Blackburn, M. L., and Hetherington, C. "The Experience of Single Women Professionals Within Student Affairs." Paper presented at the American College Personnel Association Convention, Cincinnati, March 30, 1981.

Fabe, M., and Wikler, N. *Up Against the Clock.* New York: Random House, 1979.

Faver, C. A. "Generational and Life Cycle Effects on Women's Achievement Orientation." In D. G. McGuigan (Ed.), *Women's Lives: New Theory, Research, and Policy.* Ann Arbor: University of Michigan, Center for Continuing Education of Women, 1980.

Fiske, M. "Changing Hierarchies of Commitment in Adulthood." In N. J. Smelser and E. H. Erikson (Eds.), *Themes of Work and Love in Adulthood.* Cambridge, Mass.: Harvard University Press, 1980.

George, L. K. *Role Transitions in Later Life.* Monterey, Calif.: Brooks/Cole, 1980.

George, L. K. "Models of Transitions in Middle and Later Life." *The Annals of the American Academy of Political and Social Science,* 1982, *464,* 22–37.

Giele, J. Z. "Future Research and Policy Questions." In J. Z. Giele (Ed.), *Women in the Middle Years.* New York: Wiley, 1982a.

Giele, J. Z. "Women in Adulthood: Unanswered Questions." In J. Z. Giele (Ed.), *Women in the Middle Years.* New York: Wiley, 1982b.

Giele, J. Z. "Women's Work and Family Roles." In J. Z. Giele (Ed.), *Women in the Middle Years.* New York: Wiley, 1982c.

Gilligan, C. *In a Different Voice: Psychological Theory and Women's Development.* Cambridge, Mass.: Harvard University Press, 1982.

Ginzberg, E. "Toward a Theory of Occupational Choice." In H. J. Peters and J. C. Hansen (Eds.), *Vocational Guidance and Career Development.* (2nd ed.) New York: Macmillan, 1966.

Glick, P. *American Families.* New York: Wiley, 1957.

Gould, R. L. *Transformations: Growth and Change in Adult Life.* New York: Simon & Schuster, 1978.

Gove, W. R., and Hughes, M. "Possible Causes of the Apparent Sex Differences in Physical Health: An Empirical Investigation." *American Sociological Review,* 1979, *44* (1), 126–146.

Hareven, T. K. "The Life Course and Aging in Historical Perspective." In K. W. Back (Ed.), *Life Course: Integrative Theories and Exemplary Populations.* Boulder, Colo.: Westview Press, 1980.

Hedges, J. N. "Working Women and the Division of Household Tasks." In L. S. Hansen and R. S. Rapoza (Eds.), *Career Development and Counseling of Women.* Springfield, Ill.: Thomas, 1978.

Hennig, M., and Jardim, A. *The Managerial Woman*. New York: Doubleday, 1977.

Holmstrom, L. L. "The Life Cycle of the Family." In L. S. Hansen and R. S. Rapoza (Eds.), *Career Development and Counseling of Women*. Springfield, Ill.: Thomas, 1978.

Kahn, C. "Women's Choice of a Dual Role: Brief Notes on a Developmental Determinant." In A. Roland and B. Harris (Eds.), *Career and Motherhood*. New York: Human Sciences Press, 1979.

Kangas, P. E. "The Single Professional Woman: A Phenomenological Study." Unpublished doctoral dissertation, California School of Professional Psychology, 1976.

Kanter, R. M. *Work and Family in the United States: A Critical Review and Agenda for Research and Policy*. New York: Russell Sage Foundation, 1977.

Kitagawa, E. M. "New Life-Styles: Marriage Patterns, Living Arrangements, and Fertility Outside of Marriage." *Annals of the American Academy of Political and Social Science*, 1981, *453*, 1–27.

Lehmann, T. *Adult Learning in the Context of Adult Development: Life Cycle Research and Empire State College Students*. Saratoga Springs, N.Y.: Empire State College, 1978.

Levinson, D. J. *The Seasons of a Man's Life*. New York: Knopf, 1978.

Lopata, H. *Occupation Housewife*. New York: Oxford University Press, 1971.

Lowenthal, M. F., Thurnher, M., Chiriboga, D., and Associates. *Four Stages of Life: A Comprehensive Study of Women and Men Facing Transitions*. San Francisco: Jossey-Bass, 1975.

McGuigan, D. G. "Exploring Women's Lives: An Introduction." In D. G. McGuigan (Ed.), *Women's Lives: New Theory, Research, and Policy*. Ann Arbor: University of Michigan, Center for Continuing Education of Women, 1980.

Manis, J. "Transitions to Work: Who Is Satisfied and Who Is Not?" In D. G. McGuigan (Ed.), *Women's Lives: New Theory, Research, and Policy*. Ann Arbor: University of Michigan, Center for Continuing Education of Women, 1980.

Markus, H. "Work, Women, and Well-Being: A Life Course Perspective." In D. G. McGuigan (Ed.), *Women's Lives: New Theory, Research, and Policy*. Ann Arbor: University of Michigan, Center for Continuing Education of Women, 1980.

Masnick, G., and Bane, M. J. *The Nation's Families: 1960–1990*. Cambridge, Mass.: Joint Center for Urban Studies of MIT and Harvard University, 1980.

Menaker, E. "Some Inner Conflicts of Women in a Changing Society." In A. Roland and B. Harris (Eds.), *Career and Motherhood*. New York: Human Sciences Press, 1979.

Miller, J. B. *Toward a New Psychology of Women*. Boston: Beacon Press, 1976.

Moore, K. A., Hofferth, S. L., Caldwell, S. B., and Waite, L. J. *Teenage Motherhood: Social and Economic Consequences*. Washington, D.C.: Urban Institute, 1980.

Mulvey, M. C. "Psychological and Sociological Factors in Prediction of Career Patterns of Women." *Genetic Psychology Monographs*, 1963, *68*, 309–386.

Neugarten, B. L. "Adaptation and the Life Cycle." *The Counseling Psycholgist*, 1976, *6* (1), 16–20.

Notman, M. "Midlife Concerns of Women: Implications of the Menopause." *American Journal of Psychiatry*, 1979, *136* (10), 1270–1274.

O'Rand, A. M., and Henretta, J. C. "Women at Middle Age: Developmental Transitions." *Annals of the American Academy of Political and Social Science*, 1982, *464*, 57–64.

Pearlin, L. I. "Life Strains and Psychological Distress Among Adults." In N. J. Smelser and E. H. Erikson (Eds.), *Themes of Work and Love in Adulthood*. Cambridge, Mass.: Harvard University Press, 1980.

Perun, P. J. "Comment on Rossi's 'Life-Span Theories and Women's Lives.'" *Signs*, 1981, *7* (1), 243–248.

Perun, P. J., and Bielby, D. D. V. "Structure and Dynamics of the Individual Life Course." In K. W. Back (Ed.), *Life Course: Integrative Theories and Exemplary Populations*. Boulder, Colo.: Westview Press, 1980.

Perun, P. J., and Bielby, D. D. V. "Towards a Model of Female Occupational Behavior: A Human Development Approach." *Psychology of Women Quarterly,* 1981, *6* (2), 234–252.

Plunkett, M. W. "Meanings of Work for Mothers." In D. G. McGuigan (Ed.), *Women's Lives: New Theory, Research, and Policy.* Ann Arbor: University of Michigan, Center for Continuing Education of Women, 1980.

Radloff, L. S., and Monroe, M. K. "Sex Differences in Helplessness — With Implications for Depression." In L. S. Hansen and R. S. Rapoza (Eds.), *Career Development and Counseling of Women.* Springfield, Ill.: Thomas, 1978.

Robertson, J. F. "Women in Midlife: Crises, Reverberations, and Support Networks." *Family Coordinator,* 1978, *27* (4), 375–382.

Rollins, B., and Galligan, R. "The Developing Child and Marital Satisfaction." In R. Lerner and G. Spenier (Eds.), *Child Influences on Marital and Family Interaction: A Life-Span Perspective.* New York: Academic Press, 1978.

Rossi, A. S. "Life-Span Theories and Women's Lives." *Signs,* 1980, *6* (1), 4–32.

Rubin, L. B. *Worlds of Pain.* New York: Harper and Row, 1976.

Rubin, L. B. *Women of a Certain Age.* New York: Harper and Row, 1979.

Sales, E. "Women's Adult Development." In I. H. Frieze, J. E. Parsons, P. B. Johnson, D. N. Ruble, and G. L. Zellman (Eds.), *Women and Sex Roles.* New York: Norton, 1978.

Sangiuliano, I. *In Her Time.* New York: Morrow, 1980.

Scarf, M. *Unfinished Business: Pressure Points in the Lives of Women.* New York: Doubleday, 1980.

Schlossberg, N. K. *Counseling Adults in Transition.* New York: Springer, 1984.

Serlin, E. "Emptying the Next: Women in the Launching Stage." In D. G. McGuigan (Ed.), *Women's Lives: New Theory, Research, and Policy.* Ann Arbor: University of Michigan, Center for Continuing Education of Women, 1980.

Stewart, W. R. "A Psychological Study of the Formation of the Early Adult Life Structure in Women." Unpublished doctoral dissertation, Columbia University, 1977.

Strommer, D. W. "Whither Thou Goest: Feminism and the Education of Women." *Journal of the National Association of Women Deans, Administrators, and Counselors,* 1976, *39* (2), 81–89.

Targ, D. "Toward a Reassessment of Women's Experience at Middle Age." *Family Coordinator,* 1979, *28* (3), 377–382.

Tittle, C. K. "Career, Marriage, and Family: Values in Adult Roles and Guidance." *Personnel and Guidance Journal,* 1982, *61* (3), 154–158.

Vaillant, G. E. *Adaptation to Life.* Boston: Little, Brown, 1977.

Van Dusen, R. A., and Sheldon, E. B. "The Changing Status of American Women: A Life Cycle Perspective." *American Psychologist,* 1976, *31* (2), 106–116.

Waite, L. J. *U.S. Women at Work.* Santa Monica, Calif.: Rand Corporation, 1981.

Weissman, M. M., and Klerman, G. L. "Sex Differences and the Epidemiology of Depression." *Archives of General Psychiatry,* 1977, *34* (1), 98–111.

Wells, T., and Loring, R. K. "Our Sex-Role Culture." In L. S. Hansen and R. S. Rapoza (Eds.), *Career Development and Counseling of Women.* Springfield, Ill.: Thomas, 1978.

Wiersma, J. "Women's Midlife Career Change: Facilitating the Tasks of Midlife Transition." In D. G. McGuigan (Ed.), *Women's Lives: New Theory, Research, and Policy.* Ann Arbor: University of Michigan, Center for Continuing Education of Women, 1980.

Willemsen, E. W. "Terman's Gifted Women: Work and the Way They See Their Lives." In K. W. Back (Ed.), *Life Course: Integrative Theories and Exemplary Populations.* Boulder, Colo.: Westview Press, 1980.

Young, C. M. "Work Sequences of Women During the Family Life Cycle." *Journal of Marriage and Family,* 1978, *40* (2), 401–411.

Nancy J. Evans is assistant professor of higher education and student affairs at Indiana University. She has held positions in residence life, student activities, and counseling at several colleges and universities.

Recent research on women's cognitive development is challenging the assumptions of the traditional cognitive development theories.

Cognitive Development of Women

Beverly Prosser Gelwick

Until about fifteen years ago, most of the research on cognitive and intellectual issues was subsumed under the concept of general intelligence. Since that time, there has been a great deal of research on both intellectual development and cognitive styles. Some of the earlier theorists who have influenced both of these lines of research are Lewin (1951), Erikson (1959), and Piaget (1968, 1970). As was the case in the early studies of life-span development reviewed in Chapter Two, the early work on cognitive development focused primarily on men, and the resulting theories were generalized to all adults. When women did not fit the theory, they were described as underdeveloped.

Recent research exploring women's development makes it clear that the traditional cognitive development research is inadequate. Although women have been denying the validity of the generalizations made from research on men since the 1920s (Horney, 1926, 1967 [1930]), until recently most of the critiques of the male theory of cognitive development have been ignored. Fortunately, the research of Dinnerstein (1976), Chodorow (1978), and Gilligan (1982) is now receiving attention along with the parallel critical work of women philosophers, theologians, political scientists, and literary critics.

This chapter will review research related to moral development, intellectual and ethical development, learning style, and field

N. J. Evans (Ed.). *Facilitating the Development of Women.* New Directions for Student Services, no. 29. San Francisco: Jossey-Bass, March 1985.

dependence-independence, particularly as these aspects of cognitive functioning relate to women. Studies of women's cognitive development often overlap these areas, but each will be presented separately to give a clearer picture of the work being done. Underlying the chapter are questions concerning the basic philosophical assumptions of the western research model of science.

Inadequacies in the Western Research Model

The western research model of science has elevated a distorted concept of objectivity above its natural counterpart, subjectivity, thus dichotomizing our knowing and being (Polanyi, 1958). True objectivity, as contact with reality, is distorted into an "objectivism" when subjectivity is disregarded. The objectification of knowing not only allows men's lives and experiences to be accepted as normative, it validates this limitation of human experience as scientific. Men's understanding of masculine experience shapes conceptions of "objective inquiry" in both the natural and social sciences. Urging us to respond to the crisis of our culture as human persons by transforming our understanding, R. Gelwick (1977) says, "Until the dichotomy is fought or overcome by a new philosophy that unites our knowing and being, we shall remain alien to ourselves and our world" (p. 149). Harding and Hintikka (1983) put it succinctly, "We cannot understand women and their lives by adding facts about them to the bodies of knowledge which take men, their lives, and their beliefs as the human norm.... Furthermore, it is now evident that if women's lives cannot be understood within the inherent inquiry frameworks, then neither can men's lives" (p. ix).

Cognitive Development of Women

Of the researchers suggesting that the cognitive development of women involves different factors than the cognitive development of men, Carol Gilligan has received the most attention. Her work concerning the moral development of women and the formation of women's sense of identity has received attention in the popular media as well as in professional circles. Interest in Gilligan's research has led to attempts to explain the differences between men and women (largely on the basis of socialization practices) and to a reexamination of other aspects of the cognitive development of women. Thus, investigations of intellectual and ethical development, learning style, and field dependence-independence will be reviewed here in addition to moral development research. Studies exploring specifically women's development in these areas will be highlighted.

Moral Development. Moral development was first studied by Piaget (1965 [1932]) as part of cognitive development. Observing the moral judgments that children made while practicing playing marbles, Piaget identified and described two moralities that followed one another in a developmental sequence. Preschool children through middle childhood viewed justice as obedience to authority while older children took into account the concepts of equality and reciprocity.

The next phase of moral judgment research, involving adolescents, was done by Kohlberg (Kohlberg and Kramer, 1969; Kohlberg, 1976). He identified justice as the principle central to the development of moral judgment. According to Kohlberg (1976), "moral situations are ones of conflict of perspectives or interest; justice principles are concepts for resolving these conflicts" (p. 40). To determine level of moral reasoning, Kohlberg presented the individual with a series of moral dilemmas that placed socially accepted values in conflict (Kohlberg, 1972). Kohlberg followed the development of seventy-two boys over a twenty-year period and, from the results, identified six stages that differentiated conceptions of justice. He generalized the results of this research to both men *and women,* claiming universality for his theory.

Boyd (1976) and Murphy and Gilligan (1980) found that, while Kohlberg's stage sequence described the moral development of most male students, it could not explain the judgments of women and persons (labeled "relativists") who could not make black and white, right and wrong distinctions about the dilemmas. Noting that Perry's (1968) work on intellectual and ethical development accommodated relativistic thinking, Murphy and Gilligan (1980) modified Perry's scheme to fit Kohlberg's data. The modification of theory allowed students who relied on context for interpretation and who saw truth as relative back into the revised Kohlberg theory. "This approach discovered the contextual relativism that invariably shapes the interpretation of what formerly were considered to be objective moral 'facts,' and even the facts of moral thought: It discovered that principles of justice were irreducibly tied to a contextual — that is, to a psychological and historical interpretation" (Gilligan, 1981, p. 154). Perry (1981) claims that the results of Murphy and Gilligan's work are of first-order importance in the study of moral development.

The research on moral development of women is largely influenced by the work of Dinnerstein (1976) and Chodorow (1978) who looked at the early parenting of boys and girls as they are socialized to their gender role. The fact that the principal parenting is done by the mother means that a girl is raised in an environment primarily influenced by a person of the same sex and gender identity, whereas a boy is raised by a person of the opposite sex and gender identity. Thus, girls and boys are raised in quite different environments and are taught different ways of copying, behaving, and viewing the world.

Girls are closest to an adult model of the same sex. Their gender role learning is in an intimate environment in which they must learn both to relate and to be independent. They see firsthand how a woman relates to persons of both sexes, a variety of ages, and of different family and social connections.

Boys, on the other hand, are closest to an adult of the opposite sex and not the model of choice. Their gender role learning is in both an intimate environment where they must learn "to be other," and in a lonely and unclear environment where the male model comes and goes. This, of necessity, results in a different way of moral and cognitive reasoning, which accounts for crucial differences in the personalities of women and men as well as in the way they relate to others. Chodorow (1978) contends that a fundamental reorganization of parenting is needed to change this unequal social organization. Primary parenting must be shared between men and women. Chodorow is talking at this point about the future, but Gilligan's work focuses on moral development of men and women as we see it today.

Gilligan (1981) agrees with Erikson, Piaget, Kohlberg, and others that separation and autonomy are necessary in order for men to develop a coherent sense of self and an identity as men. This developmental task is necessary to make possible the adult male capacity to love and to work. The sequential developmental ordering of identity and intimacy, however, better fits the development of men than it does women. It is impossible to fit the development of women into theories of male development without being presented with "the problem of women," or the conclusion that women are "aberrant, and outside the norm of human development," or "less than man." For women, "identity is defined in a context of relationships and is judged by a standard of responsibility and care. . . . The ethic of responsibility relies on the concept of equity, the recognition of differences in needs" (Gilligan, 1982, p. 164). Identity and intimacy are developed at the same time for women.

"Morality of rights for men is predicated on equality and centered on the understanding of fairness" (Gilligan, 1982, p. 164). Intimacy is the (adult) transformative experience for men through which adolescent identity turns into the generativity of adult love and work. When Kohlberg poses his dilemmas, he does so from an ethic that does not fit women's reality. As Miller (1976) shows, women's reality is very much organized around being able to make and then to maintain affiliations and relationships. In fact, "for many women, the threat of disruption of an affiliation is perceived not just as a loss of relationship, but as something closer to a total loss of self" (p. 83).

Gilligan changes the basic constructs for developmental theory. She shows that women's development parallels men's development, and as a result, developmental theory is expanded. Identity development now includes both individuation and interconnectedness. The moral domain now includes both fairness, and responsibility and care in relationships. "The new underlying epistemology is no longer the Greek ideal of knowledge as a correspondence between mind and form, but the Judeo-Christian ideal of knowing as a process of human relationships" (Gilligan, 1982, p. 173).

Intellectual and Ethical Development. William Perry (1968) and his associates were interested in defining the typical course of development of students' patterns of thought. In 1954, he began to document the experiences of undergraduates at Harvard and Radcliffe Colleges. From an accumulation of taped interviews with students over the four-year experience and from three samples representing different populations, Perry and his associates developed a nine-position scheme to articulate the evolution of a student's progression through college. The content of the interviews enabled a look at the interaction between intellect and identity. The students' view of the world and the nature of knowledge was explored to see how personal meaning is developed within that world. The Perry scheme traces the development of thinking about the nature of knowledge, truth and values, and the meaning of life and responsibilities.

Many researchers have consolidated Perry's nine positions into four or five positions. Although this consolidation changes Perry's scheme somewhat, the same liberty is taken here to simplify the concepts Perry presents.

Positions One and Two — Dualism: The world is seen in polar terms of *right* versus *wrong, we* versus *they.* There may be a diversity of opinion, but the Authority knows the Absolute and only needs to find the answer. Knowledge and goodness are perceived as quantitative. Dualistic students are looking for answers and expect teachers to provide them.

Position Three — Early multiplicity: Still a form of dualism, diversity and uncertainty are legitimate since Authority temporarily has not found the answer. The student in this case believes grading is based upon "good expression."

Position Four — Late multiplicity: Also a form of dualism, uncertainty is legitimate and extensive, therefore, "anyone has a right to their own opinion." However, Authority is seen to exist in a right-wrong realm in some cases. The student in this case may believe "I'm being graded on my opinion and you can't judge personal opinion." Students moving from this position are aware that Authority, in special cases, wants relativistic thinking.

A major transition occurs at this point with what Knefelkamp in conversation has called a "contextual flip." Thinking becomes qualitative; it is no longer quantitative.

Positions Five and Six—Relativism: All knowledge and values (including the authority) are contextual in relativism. Perry calls this disciplined *contextual relativism.* Dualistic thinking functions as a special case in a specific context. The student realizes the necessity of orienting oneself in a relativistic world through some sort of personal Commitment. It is important to distinguish Commitment from unquestioned and unconsidered commitment to a simple belief seen in the dualistic Authority's realm.

Positions Seven through Nine—Commitment in Relativism: Commitment is first made in one area. As the student experiences the implications of Commitment, he or she chooses a personal style (narrowness versus breadth, self-centeredness versus other-centeredness, immediacy versus detachment) and experiences an affirmation of identity among multiple responsibilities and Commitments. Commitment is an ongoing, unfolding activity through which life-style is expressed.

There are three alternatives to forward progression: (1) retreat, where the person returns to and entrenches in the dualistic or early multiplistic positions of Absolute Authority; (2) escape, where passive or opportunistic alienation provides detachment (this is seen in late multiplicity or relativism); and (3) temporizing, when a student delays in a position for a year or more exploring implications or hesitating to take the next step.

One of Perry's colleagues dubbed the growth of conceptual hierarchy that is implicit in this theory "an epistemological Pilgrim's Progress" (Perry, 1968, p. 44). The point in common is growth, a growth that implies courage, the type of courage that is defined in Tillich (1952), *The Courage to Be.* Such courage accepts a challenge to previous assumptions and allows the person to examine and enlarge himself or herself in the face of increased complexity, all the while making personal commitments. The process of learning is an enormously ego-threatening task, and Perry indicates that students consistently report that self-concept is dramatically intertwined with learning. Anyone who remembers the late adolescent years knows personally what this courage means. Using Polanyi's (1958) theory of "personal knowledge," Perry (1981) continued, "'Knowing that such and such is true' is an act of personal commitment from which all else follows. Commitments structure the relativistic world by providing focus in it and affirming the inseparable relation of the knower and the known" (p. 97).

Perry's work has provided a breakthrough in the perception of women's cognitive development. Perry understood knowledge as contextual and relative and as such questioned Kohlberg's "principled moral judgment." In "principled moral judgment," the rights of persons and ultimately the greatest justice is provided by following the highest principles, regardless of the context of the problem. Principled moral judgment is more concerned with initial rights and wrongs than it is with the consequences of an action. In the Perry scheme, this would be identified as a dualistic level of thinking. Perry says that students may develop from a stage of simplistic answers to a contextual relativism in which there are *meaningful* moral choices that are true, yet provisional. This conclusion much more closely relates to women's concern with care and responsibility. "In contrast to the man's notion of morality — 'having a reason,' 'a way of knowing what's right, what one ought to do' — is the woman's sense of morality as a type of 'consciousness,' 'a sensitivity' incorporating an injunction not to endanger or hurt other people" (Lyons, 1983, p. 126).

Reporting on the results of a longitudinal study, Clinchy and others (1977) found differential development of girls in a "traditional" and a "progressive" high school on the process and content of Commitment. Clinchy and her associates are continuing their research, looking at both the Perry and Gilligan theories in regard to the cognitive and moral development of women.

Benack (1982) modified the Perry coding scheme to allow for a finer discrimination of the separate aspects of epistemological thought. In rethinking the theoretical questions of the applicability of the Perry scheme to some women's thinking, she realized that the global coding scheme masked differences in subjects scored at the same stage, and thereby encouraged acceptance of the theory as it stands. Benack noted the particular problems that she, Gilligan, and others discovered. It appeared that many women were somewhat "relativistic" throughout their development.

> Their thought was more tolerant, more flexible at all ages than seemed to fit Perry's description of dualism. At the same time, there was not as clear evidence of self-conscious epistemological questioning and the epistemological "crisis" of multiplicity and relativism (positions four and five) in the women's data as had been observed in male samples [Benack, 1982, p. 5].

Using her new coding system with a white, middle-class, highly educated group of men and women, Benack found that the majority of the men and nearly one-third of the women scored at a single Perry position. Two-thirds of the women scored in "hybrid" categories, both dualistic and multiplistic or both dualistic and relativistic. Benack concludes that no developmental theory based on largely male samples can be assumed to reflect women's thinking.

Learning Style. Prominent in the learning style research is the work of David Kolb (1976, 1981). Kolb's "Experiential Learning Model" represents an integration of many of the intensive lines of research on cognitive style. Describing a four-stage cycle of learning, Kolb proposes (1) that concrete experience is the basis for (2) observations and reflections that lead to (3) a formation of abstract concepts and generalizations, (4) which must be tested in new situations, thereby leading to (1) a new concrete experience. To be an effective learner, one needs four abilities: (1) *concrete experience* abilities, which allow the individual to engage fully in new experiences; (2) *reflective observation* abilities, which enable the person to observe and reflect on his or her experiences; (3) *abstract conceptualization* abilities necessary to integrate experiences into concepts and theories; and (4) *active experimentation* abilities, which enable the person to use these theories in decision making and problem solving. Furthermore, learning requires a tension between the polar opposites: concrete experience versus abstract concepts and generalizations, and observations and reflections versus testing the implications of concepts in new situations. Disagreeing with Harvey, Hunt, and Schroeder (1961), who suggested that greater abstractness results in the development of more mature abilities, Kolb (1981) uses the research of Witkin and others (1962), Witkin (1976), Kris (1952), and Bruner and others (1966) to point out that both polar extremes of functioning have their costs and benefits. The dialectical model of the learning process requires both concrete and abstract abilities.

Kolb (1981) also uses the research of Kagan and Kogan (1970) who, in doing research on reflection-impulsivity, "suggest that extremes of functioning on this continuum represent opposing definitions of competence and strategies for achieving. The impulsive strategy is based on seeking reward for active accomplishment, while the reflective strategy is based on seeking reward through the avoidance of error" (p. 237).

Kolb (1981) reports several studies dealing with learning styles and different disciplines, but he does not report any sex differences. There is, in fact, no indication of sex being included as a variable. Charles Claxton and others (1982) of the Center for the Study of Higher Education at Memphis State University, who have used the Kolb Learning Style Inventory widely, also do not discuss any implications of this theory for women.

The theory is at least supportive of women's cognitive development in that it explicitly states the equal importance of the concrete with the abstract and of experience with reflection. Concrete thinking and personal experience are traditionally seen as "body" and "feminine," while reflection and abstraction are traditionally seen as "mind" and "masculine." The problem, of course, is that this polarization of masculinity and femininity is based upon a masculine view of science, which, although it sees both dimensions as necessary, reinforces the cultural view that the feminine is less valuable than the masculine.

In using the learning style inventories, one should be aware that most women likely will appear in the concrete dimension while more men will appear in the abstract dimension. The difference is likely due to the influences on cognitive development of childrearing practices mentioned earlier.

Field Dependence-Independence. Variously called field dependence versus independence (Witkin and others, 1962), global versus analytical cognitive style (Witkin, 1976), and Gestalt flexibility (Thurstone, 1944), this construct refers to individual differences in perceiving the environment. When viewing a stimulus, field-dependent people will see it as a whole, while field-independent persons will perceive the various parts of the object or situation. Two tests are used to measure this trait: the Rod and Frame Test (RFT) (Witkin and others, 1971b) and the Embedded Figures Test (EFT) (Witkin and others, 1971a). The RFT requires that subjects in a darkened room, viewing a luminous square frame with a luminous rod in its center, determine when the rod is perpendicular to the ground, regardless of the position of the frame. Individuals who can accomplish this task are termed field independent while those who are influenced by the position of the frame, resulting in errors, are labeled field dependent. For the EFT, subjects are presented with a figure hidden in a camouflaging background. Field-independent people can identify the figure easily, but field-dependent persons have more difficulty with this task.

Oetzel (1966) reports that, in eleven of thirteen studies, males were more field-independent than females. However, differences do not appear until after early childhood (Coates, 1974). Although the results of these studies have been used to suggest that men are more analytical then women, Sherman (1978) contends that the measures used to determine field independence are really tests of visual spatial perception rather than analytical ability.

Maccoby and Jacklin (1974) similarly question the experiment environment in the procedure of the Rod and Frame Test. The subject is placed in a near prone position in a dark room. They noted that a nonassertive person might not want to bother the experimenter enough to get the rod accurately adjusted. "Thus, an association between dependency and Rod and Frame performance may not have quite the meaning attributed to it, being essentially artifactual" (Sherman, 1978, p. 16f). Labeling a woman dependent or conformist as a result of the test neglects the truth that women may be uneasy in a dark room with a male stranger or that women are socialized not to be "too pushy" with men. It is safer to please than to risk potential displeasure from the experimenter, or even worse, to take possibly more of the experimenter's time than she perceives he is willing to give.

Dependence and independence are obviously important dimensions of personality, but the current measures do not show sex differences; rather, they show poor test design and implementation. It might be better to measure within gender rather then between gender. If it is possible to measure accurately global (field-dependent) students and analytical (field-independent) students, we will be able to advise them better on career choices and to institute better remedial and developmental programming. Both cognitive styles have their costs as well as their benefits and are found in both sexes.

Using Cognitive Development Theory in College Settings

There are three different scientific methodologies from which the college student affairs professional will choose in using cognitive development theory in the higher education setting. The professional can continue to use the traditional theory, as it has been developed and refined, believing that its assumptions based upon a male bias in scientific research are the best for developing new strategies for student development. For evidence that this approach is alive and well, one only needs to read Astin's (1984) new developmental theory of student involvement for higher education. This "Silver Anniversary Feature Article" in one of the most prominent journals for college student personnel workers is a compelling theory and one that many will follow. However, nowhere does Astin mention any of the recent research on women. Nor does he articulate that the developmental needs of women may be significantly different from those of men in the college years and that they may require different strategies.

The second methodology is probably the most common among student affairs professionals who are concerned with the emerging needs of men and women. Among theorists who give credence to this approach are Gilligan, Perry, and Chickering. In this approach, professionals develop strategies based upon the most recent research on women and on men to help define and articulate the needs of students.

Programming in this mode is an attempt to remedy past inequities by defending women's experience and showing a parallel development for women that is as valid as men's development.

The third methodology has its roots in the second but is radically different. This methodology questions *all theory* in western science that is not critical of the social arrangements that allow only masculine experience to determine what is objective. The authority of the "scientific expert" is questioned in this methodology. Addelson (1983) says that the work of the feminist philosophers has shown how the epistemology in our standard philosophy of science has reflected the bias of our European heritage. "Science," says R. Gelwick (1984), "despite the retreat from the absolutists' conceptions in the work of historians and philosophers of science, such as Thomas Kuhn, has continued to work as if it holds the most exact way of understanding reality" (p. 13). This third methodology uses the research of the second methodology, but cautiously. The professional is aware that the theory base is inadequate and biased and is not surprised when inconsistencies arise or when program ideas do not reflect the actual needs of students.

The following suggestions and cautions are for programming and teaching based on the new research on women's cognitive development. The first methodology is rejected. The insights of the second methodology and the basic questioning assumptions of the third methodology are explicit. With few exceptions, the cognitive development theory that underlies our profession has basic assumptions of sex difference that are consistently interwoven into the fabric of the theory and cannot be cut away or clarified without dramatically affecting the rest of the theory. In other words, one cannot dismiss Freud's view of women as parochial or culture bound while accepting as factual the remainder of his theory.

Strategies for Individuals, Groups, and Institutional Policy

In the spirit of Miller and Jones (1981), the following sections will present strategies for working with individuals, with groups, and for creating institutional policy. These strategies help students, both female and male, become self-directed in both their learning and their behavior. The most fully developed person understands that life is not primarily independent (the traditional male orientation), nor is it primarily in relationship with others (the traditional female orientation). The aim of the fully developed person is the integration of responsibility for self and for others.

Individuals. The central developmental theme for the college-age student is affirmation of self and identity clarification. College men strive to identify themselves as independent yet caring persons. Relationships with parents, teachers, and female and male friends undergo emotional and cognitive scrutiny as men focus on themselves to discover who they are as adults.

College women, on the other hand, strive to identify themselves as caring persons yet independent. Personal behavior and attitudes undergo emotional and cognitive scrutiny as women focus on relationships with parents, teachers, and female and male friends to discover who they are as adults.

As will be discussed further in Chapter Four, the prevailing social attitude in higher education now encourages women, as well as men, to plan for adult lives that include both personal career and marriage. The focus of society at best encourages women to see both as viable. Role modeling and workshops seek to portray and discuss career as possible in single and married life-styles for women. The student affairs professional must be aware that this attitude, in essence, adds women's cognitive development theory onto a masculine theory. It does not deal with women's needs as unique and thereby does not provide an opportunity for women to work through relationship issues before making personal career commitments. The issue of increased incidence of depression among college women has been widely discussed at recent annual meetings of the Association of University and College Counseling Center Directors and the American College Personnel Association. The most common problem of these depressed women appears to be an inability to integrate traditional gender-role expectation and training with the new possibilities for career and life-style patterns. The new social attitudes are simply creating a role integration problem that is often impossible for college women to resolve.

Many researchers and clinicians believe that a major cause of the current epidemic of eating disorders is a distortion of perception of body and a poor self-concept. The cultural idealization of a childlike body for women presented in the media and in the applied arts such as dance and theater in the past ten years, is a strong reinforcer. Many women with eating disorders misperceive their actual body shape. Thinking inaccurately about themselves, their body shape, and how other people see them reveals cognitive distortions that affect women's health, relationships, and studies. Evans, Bourassa, and Woolbright discuss programmatic implications of this problem in Chapter Four.

Chodorow (1978) cogently shows how women are raised to "reproduce mothering." Freud believed that women's primary purpose was to have babies and be mothers to them. He echoed the view of his time. If women must be nurturing from the time they are small children and expect to do so for the remainder of their lives, their cognitive development will reflect relationships as inherent in self-identity. For many college women, being in relationships, good or bad, is the only way self-concept is understood. It is clear, then, that the quality of and status of relationships is central to coping with all aspects of college life: educational, social, and personal.

Groups. Gilligan's (1982) conceptualization of the moral development of women indicates that differential programming for men and women is particularly important in the early college years. Gilligan identifies three levels of moral thinking. Moral decisions at level one involve caring for the self in order to ensure survival. At level two, good is equated with caring for others. At level three, the individual comes to understand that care encompasses both others and oneself. The dynamics of relationships dissipate tension between selfishness (level one) and responsibility (level two) through a new understanding of the interconnection between the self and others. Some of the adult female population reach the third level, but even these women move back and forth between levels two and three.

Programming must be designed to help women move to Gilligan's level three where they will understand that care must take into consideration the needs of both self and others. Too often women are encouraged to remain at the second level, where they take care of others rather than themselves. Programming designed to facilitate level-three thinking is especially important in coeducational living situations where women are likely to attend to the desires of their male peers rather than their own (Moos and Otto, 1975).

The new feminist thought sees women "telling their story" as central to understanding and generalizing about women. Experiences that women have thought were unique to themselves demonstrate a common thread, enabling the current cognitive researchers to see the similarity in women's development. It will be important in both individual work and in programming with women to encourage them to tell their own stories and to learn from each other.

Bernard (1981) suggests that, until the college curriculum takes sufficient account of women's experience, it will not prepare either women or men for society as we know it today. Academic learning is incomplete when the only experience it teaches is that of western white men. Komives and Evans discuss this topic in greater detail in Chapter Seven.

Institutional Policy. Bernard (1981) also criticizes the male style of administration, which is competitive and hierarchical. This style is not conducive to women faculty, student affairs staff, or students, who find competition to be threatening to relationships and too easily take a submissive role in a hierarchical structure. Whether the institution is headed by a male or a female, if cognitive development of women is to occur and the development of men is to be less bounded by an outdated masculinity, institutional policy must initiate a different style of administration. Faculty and staff must work together in an atmosphere of cooperation and trust, where interpersonal relationships are not out of reach. Komives and Evans expand on this point in Chapter Seven.

Institutional policy must begin to question the underlying assumptions of our scientific world view. Such an intellectual revolution will be long in coming and opposed by many. However, the institution and its administration and faculty who claim a mission to educate women as well as men must at least be open to reading those philosophers and natural and social scientists who are questioning the validity of an education based upon a body of knowledge that was developed by the experience of a small part of humanity.

References

Addelson, K. P. "The Man of Professional Wisdom." In S. Harding and M. Hintikka (Eds.), *Discovering Reality: Feminist Perspectives on Epistemology, Metaphysics, Methodology, and Philosophy of Science.* Boston: Riedel, 1983.

Astin, A. W. "Student Involvement: A Developmental Theory for Higher Education." *Journal of College Student Personnel,* 1984, *25* (4), 297–309.

Benack, S. "The Coding of Dimensions of Epistemological Thought in Young Men and Women." *Moral Education Forum,* 1982, *7* (2), 3–24.

Bernard, J. "Women's Educational Needs." In A. W. Chickering and Associates (Eds.), *The Modern American College: Responding to the New Realities of Diverse Students and a Changing Society.* San Francisco: Jossey-Bass, 1981.

Boyd, D. "Education Toward Principled Moral Judgment: An Analysis of an Experimental Course in Undergraduate Moral Education Applying Lawrence Kohlberg's Theory of Moral Development." Unpublished doctoral dissertation, Harvard University, 1976.

Bruner, J. S., Olver, R. R., and Greenfield, P. M. *Studies in Cognitive Growth.* New York: Wiley, 1966.

Chodorow, N. *The Reproduction of Mothering: Psychoanalysis and the Sociology of Gender.* Berkeley: University of California Press, 1978.

Claxton, C., Adams, D., and Williams, D. "Using Student Learning Styles in Teaching," *AAHE BUlletin,* 1982, *34* (9), 1.

Clinchy, B., Lief, J., and Young, P. "Epistemological and Moral Development in Girls from a Traditional and a Progressive High School." *Journal of Educational Psychology,* 1977, *69* (4), 337–343.

Coates, S. "Sex Differences in Field Independence Among Preschool Children." In R. C. Friedman, R. M. Richart, and R. L. Vande Wiele (Eds.), *Sex Differences in Behavior: A Conference.* New York: Wiley, 1974.

Dinnerstein, D. *The Mermaid and the Minotaur: Sexual Arrangements and Human Malaise.* New York: Harper Colophon Books, 1976.

Erikson, E. H. *Identity and the Life Cycle.* Psychological Issues Monograph 1. New York: International Universities Press, 1959.

Gelwick, R. L. *The Way of Discovery: An Introduction to the Thought of Michael Polanyi.* New York: International Universities Press, 1977.

Gelwick, R. L. "Liberation Theologies and the Natural Sciences." Paper presented at the meeting of the Society for Values in Higher Education, Vassar College, August 6, 1984.

Gilligan, C. "Moral Development." In A. W. Chickering and Associates (Eds.), *The Modern American College: Responding to the New Realities of Diverse Students and a Changing Society.* San Francisco: Jossey-Bass, 1981.

Gilligan, C. *In a Different Voice: Psychological Theory and Women's Development.* Cambridge, Mass.: Harvard University Press, 1982.

Harding, S., and Hintikka, M. (Eds.). *Discovering Reality: Feminist Perspectives on Epistemology, Metaphysics, Methodology, and Philosophy of Science.* Boston: Reidel, 1983.

Harvey, O. J., Hunt, D., and Schroeder, H. *Conceptual Systems and Personality Organizations.* New York: Wiley, 1961.

Horney, K. "The Flight from Womanhood: The Masculinity Complex in Women, as Viewed by Men and by Women." *International Journal of Psychoanalysis,* 1926, *7,* 324–339.

Horney, K. "The Distrust Between the Sexes." In H. Kelman (Ed.), *Feminine Psychology.* New York: Norton, 1967. (Originally published 1930.)

Kagan, J., and Kogan, N. "Individual Variation in Cognitive Processes." In P. H. Mussen (Ed.), *Carmichael's Manual of Child Psychology.* Vol 1. New York: Wiley, 1970.

Kohlberg, L. "A Cognitive-Developmental Approach to Moral Education." *Humanist,* 1972, *6* (1), 13–16.

Kohlberg, L. "Moral Stages and Moralization: The Cognitive-Developmental Approach." In T. Lickona (Ed.), *Moral Development and Behavior.* New York: Holt, Rinehart and Winston, 1976.

Kohlberg, L., and Kramer, R. "Continuities and Discontinuities in Childhood and Adult Moral Development." *Human Development,* 1969, *12* (2), 93–120.

Kolb, D. A. *The Learning Style Inventory: Technical Manual.* Boston: McBer, 1976.

Kolb, D. A. "Learning Styles and Disciplinary Differences." In A. W. Chickering and Associates (Eds.), *The Modern American College: Responding to the New Realities of Diverse Students and a Changing Society.* San Francisco: Jossey-Bass, 1981.

Kris, E. *Psychoanalytic Explorations in Art.* New York: International Universities Press, 1952.

Lewin, K. *Field Theory in Social Science.* New York: Harper & Row, 1951.

Lyons, W. P. "Two Perspectives: On Self, Relationships, and Morality." *Harvard Educational Review,* 1983, *53* (2), 125–146.

Maccoby, E. E., and Jacklin, C. N. *The Psychology of Sex Differences.* Stanford, Calif.: Stanford University Press, 1974.

Miller, J. B. *Toward a New Psychology of Women.* Boston: Beacon Press, 1976.

Miller, T. K., and Jones, J. D. "Out-of-Class Activities." In A. W. Chickering and

Associates (Eds.), *The Modern American College: Responding to the New Realities of Diverse Students and a Changing Society.* San Francisco: Jossey-Bass, 1981.

Moos, R., and Otto, J. "The Impact of Coed Living on Male and Female." *Journal of College Student Personnel,* 1975, *16* (6), 459–467.

Murphy, J. M., and Gilligan, C. "Moral Development in Adolescence and Adulthood: A Critique and Reconstruction of Kohlberg's Theory." *Human Development,* 1980, *23* (2), 77–104.

Oetzel, R. M. "Annotated Bibliography." In E. E. Maccoby (Ed.), *The Development of Sex Differences.* Stanford, Calif.: Stanford University Press, 1966.

Perry, W. *Forms of Intellectual and Ethical Development in the College Years.* New York: Holt, Rinehart and Winston, 1968.

Perry, W. "Cognitive and Ethical Growth: The Making of Meaning." In A. W. Chickering and Associates (Eds.), *The Modern American College: Responding to the New Realities of Diverse Students and a Changing Society.* San Francisco: Jossey-Bass, 1981.

Piaget, J. *The Moral Judgment of the Child.* New York: Free Press, 1965. (Originally published 1932.)

Piaget, J. *Structuralism.* New York: Harper & Row, 1968.

Piaget, J. *The Place of Sciences of Man in the System of Sciences.* New York: Harper & Row, 1970.

Polanyi, M. *Personal Knowledge: Towards a Postcritical Philosophy.* Chicago: University of Chicago Press, 1958.

Sherman, J. A. *Sex-Related Cognitive Differences: An Essay on Theory and Evidence.* Springfield, Ill.: Thomas, 1978.

Thurstone, L. *A Factoral Study of Perception.* Chicago: University of Chicago Press, 1944.

Tillich, P. *The Courage to Be.* New Haven, Conn.: Yale University Press, 1952.

Witkin, H. "Cognitive Styles in Academic Performance and in Teacher-Student Relations." In S. Messick and Associates (Eds.), *Individuality in Learning: Implications of Cognitive Styles and Creativity for Human Development.* San Francisco: Jossey-Bass, 1976.

Witkin, H. A., Dyk, R. B., Faterson, H. F. Goodenough, E. R., and Karp, S. A. *Psychological Differentiation: Studies of Development.* New York: Wiley, 1962.

Witkin, H. A., Oltman, P. K., Raskin, E., and Karp, S. A. *A Manual for the Embedded Figures Test.* Palo Alto, Calif.: Consulting Psychologists Press, 1971a.

Witkin, H. A., Oltman, P. K., Raskin, E., and Karp, S. A. *The Rod and Frame Test.* Palo Alto, Calif.: Consulting Psychologists Press, 1971b.

Beverly Prosser Gelwick is the director of the Counseling and Testing Center, University of New Hampshire. She is on the board of directors of the Society for Values in Higher Education and is president-elect of the International Association of Counseling Services, Inc.

Serving as role models, mentors, and advocates, student
affairs professionals must reconceptualize strategies to meet
the needs of young women students.

Working with Young Undergraduate Women

Nancy J. Evans, Donna M. Bourassa
Cynthia Woolbright

Today's women students have grown up in an era of the women's movement, the civil rights movement, and the Vietnam War. These events
have had an impact on them consciously or unconsciously. Consciously,
women students seek careers that are fulfilling and challenging.
Unconsciously, they remain embedded in traditional values. As Bernard points out in Chapter One, young college women are in a state of
transition characterized by the changing roles of women in society.

It is incumbent upon student affairs professionals to have an
understanding of who today's women students are. The development of
programs and services must be directed toward facilitating their
growth. This chapter provides a portrait of today's young women students, building on the information presented in Chapters Two and
Three concerning women's development. Mistakes commonly made
when programming for women are discussed, and developmental
interventions are suggested. Finally, challenges to student affairs practitioners are offered.

N. J. Evans (Ed.). *Facilitating the Development of Women.* New Directions
for Student Services, no. 29. San Francisco: Jossey-Bass, March 1985.

Portrait of the Young Undergraduate Woman

In recent years, there has been a radical shift in the composition of college students. The increased enrollment of women, particularly in the last twelve years, is one of the most significant changes. Women constitute a slight majority of today's entering students (Astin, 1984). This increase has had a far-reaching effect on college campuses; however, it has not been fully recognized.

In *The American Freshman: National Norms for Fall 1983* (Astin and others, 1983), we find that today's woman student graduated in the top 20 percent of her high school class. She is from a mostly white high school and neighborhood. She is attending college with a desire for a general education, to learn more about things, and to get a better job. She also wants to become a more cultured person. She typically resides in a residence hall. She selects her institution based primarily upon its good academic reputation with consideration for the fact that its graduates get better positions. She elects to study in a professional area with business as a second choice. She believes that women should have job equality and that minimum competence should be established for college students. Moreover, she wants to find a position in her preferred field and be satisfied with college. She has some concern over financing her college program although her parents provide the majority of support.

Differing from her male counterpart, she believes more strongly that abortion should be legalized, that busing be utilized to achieve racial balance in schools, that the death penalty should be abolished, and that there should be a national health plan. She does not support laws to prohibit homosexuality nor does she believe that women's activities should be confined to the home. She sees herself as less likely to be elected to a student office and to play varsity sports than does her male counterpart. Although she rates herself as having above average ability, she still ranks herself lower than males in academic, leadership, and mathematical ability. She is less confident intellectually and socially than the men in her class. In addition, she is generally more conservative regarding sexual issues than her male peers.

In contrast to males, today's female student is less interested in becoming an authority in her field, in being recognized by her colleagues, or in being influential in the political structure. She sees herself less likely to be financially solvent. However, she sees herself more likely than her male counterparts to influence social values, raise a family, and participate in community action through volunteerism.

In addition, she places greater emphasis on developing a philosophy of life, helping others in difficult situations, and promoting racial understanding.

This portrait of the woman student exemplifies the conflicting socialization of girls discussed in Chapter Two. In comparison to boys, they are taught to be more socially aware and more concerned about the well-being of others. They grow up with less confidence in their abilities and less desire to achieve in competitive situations. In spite of increased interest in careers, today's entering women students still maintain the "good girl" image. As Evans outlined in Chapter Two, their interests and values are reflected in their career choices, interpersonal relationships, self-image, and life-style decisions. Selected developmental issues and conflicts facing young college women within each of these areas will be examined.

Career Choices. In a review of college women's career and marriage aspirations, Blaska (1978) found that 50 to 70 percent of first-year college women and 50 to 90 percent of senior women wanted a career. In another study (Wilson and Lunneborg, 1982), no sex differences were found in the importance first-year students attached to career, marriage, and children. Career was seen as the most important aspect of life by both men and women. This pursuit of a career is a relatively new phenomenon when compared to earlier studies. For example, Empey (1958) found that female high school seniors preferred marriage to careers. While significant numbers of women remain in traditional female majors, women's choices of majors and careers span a broader range than those of men (Cook, 1981). As Evans noted in Chapter Two, many women are now entering fields that traditionally have been dominated by men. In their study of first-year college students, Wilson and Lunneborg (1982) found that 40 percent of the women had selected a nontraditional major and 30 percent were planning careers in male-dominated areas. Women were particularly attracted to business contact professions and, surprisingly, to science.

Carney and Morgan (1981) note that college women who choose nontraditional fields have higher American College Test (ACT) scores and degree expectations, are better prepared in math, come from higher family income levels, and view women's roles outside the home as less restrictive than women in traditional fields. In comparison to women who choose traditional roles, women who select careers in fields dominated by men expect to marry later and have fewer children (Tangri, 1972).

Unfortunately, women who enter nontraditional majors are

often unhappy with the paths they choose. Rea and Strange (1983) report that college women in male-dominated fields when compared to women in traditional fields were less satisfied with their chosen field and would be less likely to choose their majors again. Furthermore, they have less interaction with faculty and feel less certainty about whether they will pursue a career in their field.

Although more college women are indicating a desire to enter male-dominated fields and are majoring in nontraditional areas, a study of recent college graduates (Knight and others, 1983) found that women were still largely employed in traditional areas such as education, clerical and sales positions, and human services. They also earned significantly less than men. Compared to the men surveyed, the women were more dissatisfied with their planning and preparation for a career. The authors suggest that women may focus their attention on whether to pursue a career along with marriage rather than on choosing and planning for an appropriate career. Appley (1977) also points out that, although women are entering professional fields, they often choose less prestigious specialties, have lower aspirations for professional recognition, and rarely obtain top-level positions in their field.

While college women seem to be seriously interested in careers, research evidence suggests that they face a number of barriers to success that are not experienced by men. These include lack of confidence in their ability to be successful (Homall and others, 1975); fear of the negative consequences of competing with men (Alper, 1974; Horner, 1972); the attitudes of significant males (fathers, husbands, and boyfriends) concerning their career aspirations (Dickerson and Hinkle, 1980; Hutt, 1983); and conflicting role expectations (Rapoza and Blocher, 1978). In addition, both men and women students still perceive that their parents are more supportive of the educational goals of men than of women and that they expect male children to become leaders in their field but do not hold the same aspirations for female offspring (Dickerson and Hinkle, 1980). All of these factors may help to explain why women's actual career choices and experiences fail to match their aspirations.

Changing societal expectations of women may also help to explain these differences. McKee (1980) states:

> Women, especially those now in college, have perhaps been educated in formal and informal ways to reason that merely wanting to be a housewife is no longer an appropriate response as far as what they want to do with their lives. Television,

education, and even legislation have helped pave the way for women to become aware of and to experience job opportunities that before were not available to them. As a result, the same pressure that men have always felt to become a doctor, a lawyer, a teacher, and so on, may be affecting these college women [p. 56].

As a result, women report aspirations for nontraditional careers but in actuality enter more traditional fields or decide not to pursue a career at all.

Interpersonal Relationships. Part of the critical development process for college students is the formation of interpersonal relationships with peers, family, and faculty. As one authority states (Bernard, 1981), the interpersonal relationships of women exemplify their greater need for affiliation. The literature indicates that friendship patterns stem from one's socialization process from birth (Douvan, 1981). Men's friendships are characterized by sharing in activities, events, and projects that prepare them for competition and one-upmanship. Women's friendships, however, are based on greater intimacy, sharing, and one-to-one interactions.

Developing friendships with men that do not carry sexual overtones can be particularly problematic for young women (Douvan, 1981). Bernard (1981) suggests that:

Cross-sex friendships are discouraged in the female world, certainly among adult, especially married, women. Whether so-called platonic friendships are even possible has long been an interesting topic of debate. But when or if there are such relationships, men seem to confide more readily in women than women in men. Men, in general, are not socialized for close intimate friendship ties, least of all with women [p. 291].

Decisions concerning sexual values and intimacy also play a major role in the lives of college women (Douvan, 1981). Confusion surrounding sex role and sexual preference is an important factor among young adolescents (Sophie, 1982). One of the choices for women may be to enter into lesbian relationships (Groves and Ventura, 1983). The process of developing a lesbian identity is divided into three stages: recognizing and accepting lesbian feelings, coming out to self, and coming out to others (Sophie, 1982). Because of the ambiguities, stigmas, and stereotypes associated with a lesbian life-style, this process is a stressful life event that many women refuse to face.

Achieving resolution of the child-parent relationship is an ongoing process for eighteen- to twenty-two-year-old students. Studies indicate that women in their first year of college have a more difficult time leaving home and establishing autonomy than their male counterparts (Coons, 1976). In striving for independence, women are caught by double messages stemming from their parents' values. Parents convey both the message that "we want you to obtain a degree" and "you need an engagement ring by your senior year." Women's need for a sense of identity and reaffirmation of affection, coupled with a lack of self-trust and self-reliance, results in an elongated process of formulating adult-to-adult relationships with their parents.

For most students, meaningful relationships with faculty are rare (DeCoster and Mable, 1981). Students feel that they do not know their instructors and that their interactions with faculty are often superficial. Most noteworthy for women are the limited number of female faculty to serve as role models and mentors. They also face the fears and realities of sexual harassment from male faculty. In her article, "Taking Women Students Seriously," Rich (1979) states that incidences of sexual harassment are increasing. In a recent study (Adams and others, 1983), students indicated experiencing sexist comments (65 percent), physical advances (6 percent), sexual propositions (2 percent), and sexual bribery (2 percent). At Michigan State University, 25 percent of the women students reported sexual harassment ranging from jokes about women's anatomy to sexual assault (Mainhoff and Forrest, 1983). Few students officially report harassment; they fear reprisal, blame themselves, or assume they will not be believed (Meek and Lynch, 1983).

Self-Image. Until now, attention has been focused on "external" barriers to women's achievement. Lenney (1981) suggests that attention also be given to the "internal" or psychological barriers that contribute to women's underachievement. When Gilligan (1982) discusses concepts of self, she argues that, "While society may affirm the woman's right to choose for herself, the exercise of such choice brings her privately in conflict with the concept of femininity" (p. 70–71). This conflict causes a dilemma for women as they must reconcile their femininity and the responsibilities of adulthood. Until such reconciliation is made, women internalize these conflicts and, at times, translate them into inappropriate behaviors. The epidemic proportion of college women who suffer from compulsive eating, anorexia, and bulimia is an example of such behavior (Squire, 1983). Research shows a causal link between lack of self-esteem, poor body image, and confusion over professional goals and the rising number of eating disorders on college campuses (Kagan and Squires, 1984; Kubistant, 1982; Leclair and Berkowitz, 1983).

Poor body image is a related issue affecting significant numbers of young women who tend to avoid other issues in their lives by focusing their attention on the way their bodies look (Hooker and Convisser, 1983). Many of these women view their bodies as something separate from their person. Hooker and Convisser note that, "These women rarely, if ever, see their bodies, and even when forced to, they cannot perceive them accurately. The disgust with which they view their bodies is, for the most part, a projection of how they actually feel about themselves" (p. 237).

College women experience a greater sense of inferiority and lack of self-confidence than college men. In one study (Kagan and Squires, 1984), significant numbers of women students reported feeling inferior to others (65 percent), being too easily upset (91 percent), having difficulty expressing anger (77 percent), not being independent enough from their families (92 percent), and trying too hard to please their parents (81 percent). Nagelburg and others (1983) report that 28.9 percent of the female college students they studied suffered from serious depression.

Life-Style Decisions. As Evans pointed out in Chapter Two, there is probably no factor affecting women and men more than the current change in life-styles and role choices in relationships. Studies indicate that, in comparison to men, college women are more liberal and exhibit greater attitude change concerning sex roles (Hester and Dickerson, 1982; Wilson and Lunneborg, 1982).

College women are reporting a desire for equal marriages in which both partners work and share household responsibilities while men still prefer traditional marriage relationships where they are the primary wage earners and their wives take care of the home and family (McKee, 1980). Such differences suggest a possible source of strain in male-female relationships and marriages.

More college women intend to combine careers with marriage and children. Mash (1978) found that approximately 81 percent of the junior and senior women he surveyed planned to work at some point in addition to having children. While the majority of these women (73 percent) planned to be full-time mothers until their children entered school, 26 percent indicated that they intended to work full-time even when their children were of preschool age.

Women are also planning smaller families. Wilson (1975) found a dramatic shift after 1970. Before that year, college women consistently reported their ideal family size as four or more children; since then the preferred number of children has been two or less.

A small but significant number of college women are indicating a desire to remain single, childless, or both. Mash (1978) reports that 10 percent of the women he surveyed did not plan to marry or, if they did marry, did not intend to have children. McKee (1980) found that women aspiring to graduate degrees were more likely to report that they did not want children than those who aspired only to baccalaureate degrees.

In light of these changes in women's attitudes, Mash (1978) raises some serious questions: "What will render family and career more congruous for women, and to what extent is congruity possible? What are the implications for the role of men arising from growing numbers of women pursuing both family and career?" (p. 76).

Certainly, a number of alternative life-style arrangements, such as a more equitable division of home and child care, commuter marriages in which spouses live in different parts of the country and see each other on weekends or during vacation periods, temporary separations, and increasing divorce rates, are some results of the increasing involvement of women in careers.

Strategic Mistakes Made in Programming for Young Women

Student affairs professionals have made several strategic errors in programming for women. The first is assuming that all college women are at the same place developmentally and that all experience similar programming needs. Students exhibit different levels of awareness, understanding, and commitment in relation to issues affecting women. Programs must be provided for students possessing very traditional values and role expectations as well as those with a highly developed feminist orientation.

A second error frequently made by programmers is taking for granted that the women's movement is accepted and appreciated by young women. In an article evaluating a mentoring program for first-year college women, Taylor and McLaughlin (1982) caution:

> We found that "feminist" was an unpopular word among our female students and one with which they did not want to be associated. It became clear to us that many things achieved in the realm of women's rights during the last twenty years were taken for granted by their generation and therefore not appreciated [p. 13].

Another problem with programming for women is that it has excluded men. A significant amount of stress experienced by women occurs in their relationships with men in the workplace, in their families, and in social situations. While there is an important role to be played by programming designed exclusively for women, efforts must also be directed at raising the awareness level of men and changing their attitudes toward women.

A final error made in programming for women is the failure to institutionalize this programming thrust. Too often, women's programming rises and falls with the interest and commitment of particular staff members. Rather than relying on chance, student affairs personnel must ensure that they have institutional support, mechanisms for accountability, and a coherent, ongoing program.

Suggested Developmental Interventions

The development of young women is most effectively encouraged by systematic efforts consisting of individual advisement and counseling, programming for groups, and environmental intervention. Interventions should focus on increasing knowledge, changing attitudes, and developing needed skills. Such efforts can be structured around the four main developmental areas presented in Chapter Two: career choice, interpersonal relationships, self-concept, and life-style decisions.

Career Choice. Individual career counseling should focus on self-assessment. Young women should be encouraged to clarify their interests, values, and skills in relation to the world of work. Counselors have a responsibility to validate traditional as well as nontraditional career choices and decisions not to pursue careers. Young women must also be helped to recognize that career decision making is an ongoing process, not a one-time decision.

Career development programming should provide information about the world of work and assist women in developing attitudes and skills necessary to succeed. For example, seminars that explore stereotypes and attitudes held within various professions can provide women with a fuller understanding of the occupational field they select. The recognition and understanding of power, negotiation, and influence are significant factors in organizational cultures. Leadership courses, seminars, and conferences should be offered focusing on issues such as assertiveness, power, supervising men, persuasive communication, and networking. Attention must also be given to advancement strategies for women in their careers. The opportunity to interact with and learn from women holding various professional positions is particularly important in providing a realistic picture of the professional work atmosphere.

Since women often fail to take advantage of voluntary programming activities, we must begin building career development programs into the formal curriculum. General career development courses should deal with issues that affect women's career decision making and with conditions in the workplace that affect women. Such information appropriately raises the awareness of male students as well as women.

Faculty, especially those in fields traditionally dominated by males, should be encouraged to assist in the development of programs concerning career issues facing women in their areas. Faculty members can often present a more accurate picture of careers in their fields to women than student affairs professionals. Researching and presenting such a program also has the added benefit of heightening the faculty member's awareness concerning the needs of women students.

The development of formal and informal mentoring relationships should be encouraged. Again, faculty assistance can be enlisted in establishing such programs. Involvement of professional women in the community and of alumni should also be investigated.

Finally, women should be encouraged to take advantage of fieldwork and internship opportunities. These types of work experiences give young women a realistic picture of the fields they are considering and the skills they will need to succeed.

Interpersonal Relationships. Students must be assisted in developing their values and skills in relation to other people, and the institution must provide an environment in which healthy relationships can be developed. Individual counseling and advising can help young women examine their sexual values and the needs that relationships fulfill in their lives. Provision must also be made for counseling victims of sexual assault (past or present) and sexual harassment.

Examination of sex roles, male-female relationships, and communication patterns is particularly effective in group settings. It is often helpful to have participants do some exploration in same-sex groups and then come together in mixed-sex groups to discuss their ideas and try out new behaviors. Requiring students living on coed residence hall floors to enroll in a class on sociology of sex roles is another interesting programming idea (Buckner, 1981). Rape awareness programs designed to educate both women and men are also an important aspect of any comprehensive programming for women.

Some students can benefit from support groups organized to discuss relationships with parents. Young women often provide each other with creative ideas and support for becoming more independent and self-confident in their interactions with parents.

Institutions have a responsibility to take a strong, public stand against sexual harassment including in-service training for administrators and supervisors, support for students and staff reporting instances of harassment, and education for the entire campus community. The program at Michigan State University (Simon and Forrest, 1983) is an excellent prototype.

Escort services also deserve institutional support. Too often these programs are developed by student organizations that have difficulty maintaining a reliable service. Women have the right to safe travel and use of campus facilities at night.

Programs that encourage positive, informal interaction between faculty and women students are badly needed. At Indiana University, the Briscoe Fellows program pairs faculty members with residence hall floors. Faculty members visit the floor, participate in and help plan floor activities, and informally advise students on career decisions, course selection, and job searches. A special effort should be made to pair women faculty and students in such programs.

Self-Concept. Student affairs staff must be prepared to assist women students experiencing depression, stress, low self-esteem, concerns about body image, mild to severe eating disorders, and other issues related to self-concept. Often such issues require that women be referred to highly trained counselors who can work with them on a long-term basis. Women suffering from anorexia and bulimia, for instance, seem to respond best to a combination of long-term individual therapy, family therapy, and group treatment. Such treatment raises important issues for counseling center staff who often face pressure from administrators to offer only short-term treatment. Institutions have an obligation either to offer the services needed by the women on their campuses or to see that such services are available at reasonable cost in the community. Student services staff must be trained to recognize students with emotional problems and make appropriate referrals.

Support groups are an effective programming tool to assist students experiencing less severe self-concept concerns. As Evans noted in Chapter Two, peer interaction and validation is particularly important to women and can offset many of the negative messages they give themselves.

Life-Style Decisions. As with other career decisions, student affairs staff have an obligation to help women students explore various life-styles and to support whatever decisions seem appropriate for them. Women should be presented with information on various life-styles including dual-career marriages, singleness, lesbianism, childless marriages, as well as more traditional life-style alternatives. Both the positive and negative aspects of these options need to be explored.

Role models are especially valuable as women consider various alternatives. Programs that expose women to individuals who have made a variety of life-style choices are needed. Staff, faculty, and community women can be called on to participate in workshops, seminars, and informal discussions concerning life-style alternatives and the decisions they have made in their lives.

Responsibilities of Student Affairs Professionals

If programming for women is to be successful, we must begin by assessing our own attitudes, values, and beliefs about women. Men and women professionals alike must question and challenge themselves in these areas. In addition, we must review our programs and services in counseling, student union activities, residence halls, athletics, and other departments. Our responsibilities include:

- Serving as role models and mentors
- Establishing clear goals and priorities for recruitment and retention of women professionals
- Initiating women's programs
- Counseling women in an environment free of sex bias
- Advocating for change to support women's full participation in the institution.

Komives and Evans develop these ideas further in Chapter Seven.

Summary

There are no easy solutions to these complex issues and concerns. Our success lies in the institutional and individual commitment to take responsibility for reshaping the educational process. Women are a diverse and complex group. Our programs and services must reflect this diversity. We must take an active role in creating an environment in which the transmission of sexist ideologies is eliminated. This is our responsibility to the next generation.

References

Adams, J. W., Kottke, J. L., and Padgitt, J. S. "Sexual Harassment of University Students." *Journal of College Student Personnel,* 1983, *24* (6), 484–490.

Alper, T. G. "Achievement Motivation in College Women: A Now-You-See-It-Now-You-Don't Phenomenon." *American Psychologist,* 1974, *29* (3), 194–203.

Appley, D. G. "The Changing Place of Work for Women and Men." In A. Sargent (Ed.), *Beyond Sex Roles.* New York: West Publishing, 1977.

Astin, A. W. "A Look at Pluralism in the Contemporary Student Population." *NASPA Journal,* 1984, *21* (3), 2–12.

Astin, A. W., and others. *The American Freshman: National Norms for Fall 1983.* Los Angeles: Cooperative Institutional Research Program, Graduate School of Education, University of California, 1983.

Bernard, J. *The Female World.* New York: Free Press, 1981.

Blaska, B. "College Women's Career and Marriage Aspirations: A Review of the Literature." *Journal of College Student Personnel,* 1978, *19* (4), 302–305.

Buckner, D. R. "Developing Coed Residence Hall Programs for Sex-Role Exploration." *Journal of College Student Personnel,* 1981, *22* (1), 52–59.

Carney, M., and Morgan, C. S. "Female College Persisters: Nontraditional Versus Traditional Career Fields." *Journal of College Student Personnel,* 1981, *22* (5), 418–423.

Cook, E. P. "Sex Differences in the Career Choices of College Students." *Journal of College Student Personnel,* 1981, *22* (3), 256–261.

Coons, F. "The Developmental Tasks of the College Student." In D. DeCoster and P. Mable (Eds.), *Student Development and Education in Residence Halls.* Washington, D.C.: American College Personnel Association, 1976.

DeCoster, D., and Mable, P. (Eds.). *Understanding Today's Students.* New Directions for Student Services, no. 16. San Francisco: Jossey-Bass, 1981.

Dickerson, K. G., and Hinkle, D. E. "Entering College Freshman Still Perceive That Their Parents View Men's Achievement as More Important — A Self-Perpetuating View?" *Journal of College Student Personnel,* 1980, *20* (4), 344–349.

Douvan, E. "Capacity for Intimacy." In A. W. Chickering and Associates (Eds.), *The Modern American College: Responding to the New Realities of Diverse Students and a Changing Society.* San Francisco: Jossey-Bass, 1981.

Empey, L. T. "Role Expectations of Women Regarding Marriage and a Career." *Marriage and Family Living,* 1958, *20* (2), 152–155.

Gilligan, C. *In a Different Voice: Psychological Theory and Women's Development.* Cambridge, Mass.: Harvard University Press, 1982.

Groves, P. A., and Ventura, L. A. "The Lesbian Coming-Out Process: Therapeutic Considerations." *The Personnel and Guidance Journal,* 1983, *62* (3), 146–149.

Hester, S. B., and Dickerson, K. G. "The Emerging Dual-Career Life-Style — Are Your Students Prepared for It?" *Journal of College Student Personnel,* 1982, *23* (6), 514–519.

Homall, G. M., Juhasz, S., and Juhasz, J. "Differences in Self-Perception and Vocational Aspirations of College Women." *California Journal of Educational Research,* 1975, *26* (1), 6–10.

Hooker, D., and Convisser, E. "Women's Eating Problems: An Analysis of a Coping Mechanism." *Personnel and Guidance Journal,* 1983, *62* (4), 236–239.

Horner, M. "The Motive to Avoid Success and Changing Aspirations of College Women." In J. M. Bardwick (Ed.), *Readings on the Psychology of Women.* New York: Harper & Row, 1972.

Hutt, C. H. "College Students' Perceptions of Male and Female Career Patterns." *Journal of College Student Personnel,* 1983, *24* (3), 240–246.

Kagan, D. M., and Squires, R. L. "Compulsive Eating, Dieting, Stress, and Hostility Among College Students." *Journal of College Student Personnel,* 1984, *25* (3), 213-220.

Knight, G. D., Sedlacek, W. E., and Bachhuber, T. D. "Occupational Status and Career Development Needs of Recent Female College Graduates." *Journal of College Student Personnel,* 1983, *24* (2), 152–156.

Kubistant, T. "Bulimarexia." *Journal of College Student Personnel,* 1982, *23* (4), 333–339.

Leclair, N. J., and Berkowitz, B. "Counseling Concerns for the Individual with Bulimia." *Personnel and Guidance Journal,* 1983, *61* (6), 352–355.

Lenney, E. "What's Fine for the Gander Isn't Always Good for the Goose: Sex Differences in Self-Confidence as a Function of Ability Area and Comparison with Others." *Sex Roles: A Journal of Research,* 1981, *7* (9), 905–924.

McKee, S. F. "Marriage Life-Style Plans, Educational Aspirations, and Career Decision Making Among Male and Female Undergraduates." Unpublished master's thesis, Bowling Green State University, 1980.

Maihoff, N., and Forrest, L. "Sexual Harassment in Higher Education: An Assessment Study." *Journal of the National Association for Women Deans, Administrators, and Counselors,* 1983, *46* (2), 3-8.

Mash, D. J. "The Development of Life-Style Preferences of College Women." *Journal of the National Association for Women Deans, Administrators, and Counselors,* 1978, *41* (2), 72-76.

Meek, P. M., and Lynch, A. Q. "Establishing an Informal Grievance Procedure for Cases of Sexual Harrassment of Students." *Journal of the National Association for Women Deans, Administrators, and Counselors,* 1983, *46* (2), 30-33.

Nagelburg, D. B., Pillsbury, E. C., and Balzer, D. M. "The Prevalence of Depression as a Function of Gender and Facility Usage in College Students." *Journal of College Student Personnel,* 1983, *24* (6), 525-529.

Rapoza, R. A., and Blocher, D. H. "A Comparative Study of Academic Self-Estimates, Academic Values, and Academic Aspirations of Adolescent Males and Females." In L. S. Hansen and R. S. Rapoza (Eds.), *Career Development and Counseling of Women.* Springfield, Ill.: Thomas, 1978.

Rea, J. S., and Strange, C. C. "The Experience of Cross-Gender Majoring Among Male and Female Undergraduates." *Journal of College Student Personnel,* 1983, *24* (4), 356-362.

Rich, A. *On Lies, Secrets, and Silence.* New York: Norton, 1979.

Simon, L. A. K., and Forrest, L. "Implementing a Sexual Harrassment Program at a Large University." *Journal of the National Association for Women Deans, Administrators, and Counselors,* 1983, *46* (2), 23-29.

Sophie, J. "Counseling Lesbians." *The Personnel and Guidance Journal,* 1982, *60* (6), 341-345.

Squire, S. "Is the Binge-Purge Cycle Catching?" *Ms. Magazine,* 1983, *12* (4), 41-46.

Tangri, S. S. "Determinants of Occupational Role Innovation Among College Women." *Journal of Social Issues,* 1972, *28* (2), 177-199.

Taylor, I. C., and McLaughlin, M. B. "Mentoring Freshmen Women." *Journal of the National Association of Women Deans, Administrators, and Counselors,* 1982, *45* (2), 10-15.

Wilson, K. M. "Today's Women Students: New Outlooks and New Challenges." *Journal of College Student Personnel,* 1975, *16* (5), 376-381.

Wilson, V. M., and Lunneborg, P. W. "Implications of Women's Changing Career Aspirations for College Counselors." *Journal of College Student Personnel,* 1982, *23* (3), 236-239.

Nancy J. Evans is assistant professor of higher education and student affairs at Indiana University. She has held positions in residence life, student activities, and counseling at several colleges and universities.

Donna M. Bourassa is currently a coordinator of residence life and part-time instructor in the School of Education at Indiana University. She serves as a chairperson of the Personal Liberation Task Force Committee for the Department of Residence Life.

Cynthia Woolbright is presently the director of student activities/student center at Bentley College. She is president-elect of the Association of College Unions — International.

*The continuing increase in the numbers of adult women
returning to higher education will require all institutions
to reexamine their policies and provide additional support
programs and services.*

Addressing the Concerns of Returning Women Students

Gay Holliday

The 1980s will call upon American higher education to meet one of its greatest challenges — the challenge of meeting the needs of a student body composed of a significant number of adult women returning to colleges and universities. Once perceived as a woman who enrolled to alleviate boredom or to take an occasional enrichment course, the returning woman is now viewed by institutions as a serious student. The total number of college students declined in 1978, and at the same time older students increased more than 21 percent (Saslaw, 1981). Two-thirds of these older students are women. Institutions must realize the needs of their new clientele and develop new goals, policies, and support programs. This chapter will explore the characteristics of re-entry women and their reasons for returning to higher education; it will also discuss life-span development as it relates to adult women, review obstacles confronting women as they return to higher education, and offer recommendations to institutions concerning policy changes and the development of support services specifically designed to serve better the needs of returning women.

A Profile of Returning Women

Demographics. A growing trend in higher education in the 1970s and 1980s is the movement toward adult education. The tremendous

N. J. Evans (Ed.). *Facilitating the Development of Women.* New Directions
for Student Services, no. 29. San Francisco: Jossey-Bass, March 1985.

rise in the number of mature women returning to education is well documented. These women are referred to as "re-entry women" because they usually are returning to formal education after an interruption. In 1972 a total of more than 1.1 million women students over the age of twenty-five were enrolled in higher education. Of these, 627,000 were over twenty-five years of age, and 475,000 were age thirty-five years or older. The average age of re-entry women is between thirty-six and forty, with the age span between twenty-four and eighty years of age (Molstad, 1984). Molstad further cites Census Bureau estimates that, in 1985, 40 percent of all college students will be older than twenty-five years of age.

Characteristics. Benjamin (1979) reviewed various studies conducted by Astin (1976) and others that provide a profile of the returning adult woman student. She is generally in her thirties or forties, married, and a housewife with children. She is usually white and from the middle class, with some college experience before marriage. She has a history of paid work and/or volunteer experience, and she is financially stable. These generalizations should be noted with caution because they do not take into account the diversity of the re-entry woman population or recognize the subgroups that exist due to individual statuses, life cycle stages, and personal characteristics. Benjamin further cites Tittle and Denker (1980) who recognize subcategories and isolate three sets of variables as important:

1. Sex role, marital status, and family status, including the number and ages of children
2. Occupation or career status, including past and present financial needs
3. Individual characteristics likely to influence reasons for attending, levels of career aspiration, and values relating to sex and occupational roles.

The re-entry woman today is no longer just the middle-class, middle-income, middle-aged woman with time on her hands for enrichment courses. Re-entry women are represented more and more by minority, lower-income women who are single parents and heads of households and single women interested in career advancement. These women are serious, determined, enthusiastic, highly motivated, eager to learn, and academically successful.

Reasons for Returning. A review of the research (Brandenburg, 1974; Karelius-Schumacher, 1977; Scott, 1980; Tittle and Denker, 1980) focusing on the reasons a woman re-enters higher education reveals several major themes:

- Economic necessity, either adding to the financial base of her family or gaining financial independence

- Preparation for a career or occupation
- Need for intellectual fulfillment, satisfaction, and realization of her potential
- More time to devote to her own interests because less time is needed for childcare
- Preparation for a career change
- Enhancement of skills and abilities to increase job options
- Divorce or death of a spouse
- Increased appetite for education
- Enrollment in an advanced degree program
- Desire for increased status as a college graduate.

Markus (1973) reports that there is a temporal cycle in achievement motives associated with the ages and family situations of college-educated women. There is a period of low achievement needs corresponding to high family involvement. When the family is grown, there is a return to previous high achievement need levels. The return to school is motivated by a need for individual achievement in other than interpersonal areas. The Markus study found that the majority of re-entry women were interested in enlarging their own interests and in increasing their own skills.

Developmental Issues in the Lives of Re-Entry Women

As noted in Chapter Two, the study of human development has taken on a new emphasis, with increased attention devoted to growth and development during the adult years. The life-span perspective can be especially useful in an examination of the re-entry adult woman since it emphasizes that development occurs at all points in life and within the total context of the individual's world (Deutsch and Hultsch, 1981). A number of issues are particularly salient for this group of women.

Letchworth (1970) conceptualizes motivation for women returning to college in terms of an identity-integrity conflict. The identity conflict refers to the period when a woman questions her abilities, limitations, cultural values, and attitudes while attempting to attain an occupation or a suitable role in society. This identity crisis may be somewhat resolved when a woman becomes a mother but tends to reoccur after children are grown. The integrity crisis includes questions of, "How can I relate to the world?" It requires active participation, and, if resolved, it leads a woman to more individualized relations with herself, others, and society. She becomes interested in a style of life that is significant and meaningful.

Astin (1976) also points out that adult women in higher education are searching for integrity and identity. She states that women's coping styles in later life differ from men's because women show a greater need for independence and are more outgoing and assertive. They also remove themselves from the nurturing roles they previously accepted. Astin further states that these observed sex differences in adult behavior can assist in understanding women's need for redirection, accomplishment, and a work orientation. As a result of their redefinition of themselves in terms of new roles and experiences, returning women typify adult learners: They are aware of reasons for learning and understand the benefits of education.

Current developmental theories are most often applied to the traditional undergraduate student who is seventeen to twenty-two years old, but some aspects may be helpful when thinking about the development through which an individual progresses in sequence: achieving competence, managing emotions, becoming autonomous, establishing identity, freeing interpersonal relationships, clarifying purposes, and developing integrity. A mature woman returning to higher education will probably have moved successfully through several of the vectors, but once she enters a new environment (the campus setting), she may begin recycling through these developmental tasks.

Her feelings of competence may be lowered. Her emotional well-being may fluctuate. She may be striving for autonomy in a different way and may be attempting to establish a new identity. This recycling process can contribute initially to a disruption in her functioning. The length of the recycling process will be dependent upon the level of her cognitive development and life experiences. It can also be shortened by providing adequate institutional support systems to assist her in her transition into the environment.

Astin (1976) notes that the existing literature has focused on the developmental differences between youth and adulthood and between adult men and adult women. So far, no attempt has been made to differentiate among groups of women on the basis of their past roles and experiences. Most of the literature centers on women whose primary roles have been as wives and mothers. The similarities and differences between these women and women who have made career commitments have not been examined.

Similarly, most studies of women in adult education programs have focused on women in search of identity and integrity, who have new outwardly directed goals, who require more assertive behaviors, and who are actively assimilating new experiences. Only a few studies have included women who have always been career oriented and who have returned to update their skills or to develop new skills in pursuit of second careers. More information on these women is needed.

Barriers to Re-Entry

Tittle and Denker (1980) identify issues that hinder a woman's return to higher education from three major perspectives: (1) how the institution deals with her, (2) personal circumstances affecting her, and (3) her concept of herself and her world. Furthermore, they cite studies that categorize the barriers re-entry women face as institutional, situational, and dispositional.

Institutional. Some of the institutional factors that have excluded women are sex and age quotas, financial aid, admission policies, stringent curriculum planning and course scheduling, inadequate support services such as childcare, and faculty and staff attitudes (Tittle and Denker, 1980). Although discrimination in admissions is prohibited under Title IX of the Education Amendments of 1972, private institutions, some religious institutions, and military academies are exempted. In addition, the differing data on ability levels of male and female students enrolled suggest that some forms of age and sex discrimination still exist, particularly related to re-entry women. As more women complete their education and enter the labor market to utilize their degrees, attitudes should begin to change.

A more serious barrier is the discrimination against part-time re-entry women. Institutions still prefer full-time students, even though the need for students has lessened the stricture on part-time enrollment. However, many institutions have regulations concerning full-time course loads and degree completion periods that particularly hinder low-income women or women with children.

Existing forms of financial aid for re-entry women do not meet their needs. Most financial aid is unavailable to them and is restricted to full-time students. Additionally, information concerning financial aid is not always easily accessible to them. As a result, many women who could successfully re-enter higher education do not do so because they do not have the necessary financial resources.

Course scheduling and admissions regulations may also provide barriers. While attempts are being made to provide increasing flexibility in order to help maintain enrollments, few efforts have been made to examine the scheduling and cycling of classes for part-time students (Tittle and Denker, 1980). Problems also exist in evaluating outdated transcripts and in the transfer of credits that may have been earned several years earlier. Securing letters of recommendation may be a barrier for a woman who has been out of school for several years.

The availability of childcare facilities, or rather their lack of availability, has been cited as the single most critical problem for returning women (Tittle and Denker, 1980). Surveys routinely find that a majority of women with children will state that their academic work is hampered by the need for childcare. In one survey, 57 percent of women in graduate school stated that "excellent daycare facilities were essential to their going to graduate school, as well as the possibility of matriculating as a part-time student" (Tittle and Denker, 1980, p. 441). The need varies with the age of the children. Childcare is more readily available for preschool children, but it often ends at the time of day when it is difficult to arrange for other care. School-age children need services after school, and alternatives for care are limited. Most women rely on childcare facilities in the community because institutionally supported or sponsored facilities are limited or nonexistent.

Faculty and staff attitudes are often based on sex stereotypes and are likely to be subtle; they frequently take the form of lesser expectations of women in terms of career development and job placement (Tittle and Denker, 1980). Plotsky (1975) studied the attitudes of faculty at the University of Texas-Austin, toward students twenty-five years of age and older. The following statements reflect consensus by the faculty surveyed:

1. Pursuing a master's degree is all right at any age, but age is a factor for consideration by those wishing to pursue a Ph.D.
2. Adults need a longer period of time to adjust to college than the traditional student.
3. Older students are dominating in class (especially older veterans and retired officers).
4. Older students have other responsibilities that interfere or "occupy the mind."
5. Older students do better work than the traditional student.
6. Older students are "too reticent" in class discussion.
7. Older students do not fit into the academic framework of UT-Austin (may not become a true scholar).
8. Older students provide a different viewpoint from the typical student.
9. Older students may need extra conference time for help on a Ph.D., professional choices, degree choices, or explanation of course material [p. 22].

These statements may be somewhat representative of faculty and staff perceptions of older students at other institutions. The absence of female role models among university faculty and staff is another frequently cited barrier.

Situational. Social and situational barriers are obvious in two major areas: external forces with which the woman who returns to higher education must contend, and barriers that arise from the social class and ethnic or racial group to which the returning student belongs.

Tittle and Denker (1980) cite research indicating that fewer women from lower socioeconomic groups are likely to participate in higher education than males from these groups. Traditional sex-role attitudes still exist among working-class families, and there is less expectation that women will continue their education. The authors cite research suggesting that "with the exception of black women, the college attendance rate of minority women is under that of both males of all ethnic groups and white (majority) females" (Tittle and Denker, 1980, p. 42).

Society places a value on youth that makes the older returning student initially feel physically, socially, and psychologically out of place. As a result, these students may experience a heightened sense of aging or may develop a general sense of worthlessness (Scott, 1980). Because of the value placed on work in this nation, a return to school may be seen as being in conflict with the individual's role as a productive contributor to society.

Emphasis is also placed on involvement in the community. By returning to school, the adult woman is often forced to disinvolve herself from community affairs, which could lead to a loss of status. A return to school may also be accompanied by a reduction in economic status. Other situational factors affecting returning women include marital status, mobility, access to financial support, and geographic location.

Psychological. Psychological barriers encompass diverse topics: attitudes toward appropriate roles for women; the socialization process and development of female identity; and questions concerning the returning woman's needs, concerns, and family attitude. These barriers can be culturally and experientially based, but common elements for all women are the variables that relate to the development of feminine identity centered primarily on the wife and mother roles and the accompanying delay in other definitions of self (Tittle and Denker, 1980).

A number of studies report that major problems occur in terms of management of time and family responsibilities (Scott, 1980). Spending less time with children, husband, and friends, and neglecting housework creates problems for many returning women. In addition, women face problems in the area of family conflicts and in not having enough time for study, recreation, and planning. Difficulties in the adjustment of one's schedule to include academic and household responsibilities is evident. Many women report as a problem the management of guilt related to the multiple roles.

Many women also have anxiety about their abilities as well as about their decision to return to school. They experience lack of self-confidence as they initially perceive themselves to be in competition with bright, young students. As a result, many develop a poor self-image.

Viewed from the life-cycle perspective, women who return to higher education in their twenties and early thirties, who are married, and who have young children face different psychological barriers than women who return in their forties or later, who are married, and who have children at or near ages when they will leave home. These two groups of women probably comprise between 80 and 90 percent of the returning women in any institution.

The first group of women in their twenties and early thirties are likely to have younger children, and great demands may be placed upon them to fulfill adequately their multiple roles as mother, wife, homemaker, and student. This group's most significant psychological barrier may be the guilt they feel related to the amount of time spent with their children (Tittle and Denker, 1980). If family and friends are not accepting and supportive in their decision to return to school, women in this group are most likely not to continue their education.

Women in their forties or older most likely have grown children who may not live at home. Their guilt may center on feelings of relief that they no longer have to devote as much time to their children and that they now have time for themselves (Tittle and Denker, 1980). These women become more concerned with developing an identity and with decisions that will affect the rest of their lives.

The success of a re-entry woman with a husband and children is often dependent upon their acceptance and support as well as on the support of her friends. The support may be verbalized, but the feelings behind it may be ambivalent. A woman may feel guilty about using family monies to support her education and about asking the family to assume more responsibility in the home. If the husband is not supportive, a power struggle may develop in which he withdraws his acceptance. Encouragement from her husband and children can aid in easing many of the psychological barriers a woman faces.

Support Services

In spite of the obstacles facing the adult woman's return to higher education, it appears to be a valuable and positive experience (Scott, 1980). The ease of the transition is directly dependent upon the institution's recognition of the specific needs of this population and its provision of adequate programs and support services. In order to evaluate an institution's commitment to returning women, Tittle and Denker (1980) suggest that the following must be checked to determine if programs are specifically designed for returning women:

- Financial aid
- Recruitment program

- Accessible class location and flexible class scheduling
- Evening and weekend hours for offices providing support services such as counseling, advising, etc.
- Childcare facilities and referral to childcare services
- Social functions
- Life experience credit
- Women's center or development of support groups
- Career development planning
- Curriculum offerings to enhance skills in writing, math, studying, taking exams, etc. [p. 157].

Institutional commitment and support for re-entry women across the country is uneven, but the number of returning women clearly points to the need for all institutions to make some changes and adopt more flexible policies to accommodate individual differences within the student populations they serve. Institutions must examine their existing support services and determine what additional services should be added.

Some Specific Recommendations

The following recommendations are offered to assist institutions in developing and strengthening support services for re-entry women.
Recruitment.
1. Develop a specific recruitment program for undergraduate and graduate re-entry women, and train specified personnel in admissions to be responsive to the needs of this special population.
2. Develop information specifically designed for re-entry women. Include information on financial aid, childcare, counseling, and support services that are available.
3. Actively engage in community outreach programs that identify potential re-entry women and provide the appropriate agencies with information.
4. Develop recruitment presentations on campus specifically designed for returning women.
Admissions.
1. Review regulations that require transcripts of previous work, entrance exams, and letters of recommendation for women who have been out of education for a number of years.
2. Develop procedures for awarding credit for demonstration of competency equivalency and life credit. Make re-entry women aware of the alternatives of the College-Level Examination Program (CLEP) and the College Proficiency Examination Program (CPEP).

3. Review residency requirements in determining tuition status. Residency should not be based upon the status of the spouse.

4. Simplify admissions procedures and be more flexible in applying admissions policies to re-entry women.

Orientation.

1. Develop ongoing orientation programs designed for re-entry women. Programs should be offered prior to enrollment, in the summer and at the beginning of each academic semester. Programs should offer information about the services designed for returning women and serve to facilitate the development of a support network.

2. Throughout the academic year, offer specific workshops for returning women on topics such as sex roles, improving self-concept, time management, career interests, and leadership skills.

3. Include orientation sessions for spouses, children, and significant others involved with re-entry women.

4. Develop an orientation handbook designed for re-entry women.

Financial Aid. Many researchers (Dunkle, 1980; Scott, 1980; Creange, 1980) have made practical recommendations in the area of financial aid. Some of these recommendations include:

1. Evaluate financial aid policies and practices to determine if they are in compliance with the Title IX Education Amendments of 1972 and the Age Discrimination Act of 1975.

2. Determine if financial aid is readily available to re-entry women even if they are enrolled part-time.

3. Revise policies and practices to ensure that financial aid information highlights eligibility for re-entry women.

4. Ensure that scholarship funds, low-income loans, short-term loans, and crisis loans are available.

5. Ensure that re-entry women have access to fellowships.

6. Distribute financial aid information through nontraditional sources.

7. Establish tuition deferral systems to include credit or installment payments.

8. Provide information on how re-entry women can reduce costs, such as purchasing used books and using educational expenses as tax deductions.

9. Revise the standard "need" formula.

10. Provide cost breaks, such as family tuition plans.

11. Unbundle tuition costs to include only course costs.

12. Assist in the reduction of childcare costs through financial aid.

13. Provide more equal treatment in giving financial aid to students who are financially independent.

14. Alter the financial aid guidelines so women's qualifications are not entirely based on their husbands' income.

15. Offer opportunities for work study and paid internships.

Professional Staff.

1. Train admissions and recruitment staff to be sensitive to the needs of re-entry women, and identify specific persons to provide financial aid information.

2. Train peer counselors to assist returning women.

Childcare. Maes (1979) and Scott (1980) suggest the following:

1. Provide college-sponsored or college-supported childcare facilities.

2. Provide lists of nearby childcare resources.

3. Develop strategies to reduce childcare costs.

4. Assist women in "pooling" their resources so they can help each other with childcare responsibilities.

5. Ensure that information about adequate health care facilities for children in the community is available.

Counseling. Scott (1980), Maes (1979), Saslaw (1981), and Astin (1976) offer the following recommendations:

1. Select and retrain counseling specialists to assist re-entry women.

2. Provide and facilitate ongoing support groups.

3. Provide personal counseling in the areas of multiple roles, role overload, and role strain.

4. Provide workshops on self-awareness, feminine issues, and self-exploration.

5. Train peer counselors to assist re-entry women.

6. Provide basic skill-building seminars on topics such as how to study and test anxiety.

7. Provide marital and family counseling.

8. Present seminars on strategies for coping with change and stress.

9. Ensure flexible hours when counseling services are available.

10. Expand educational and vocational counseling for returning women.

11. Utilize the business and industrial community to provide information about career opportunities for re-entry women.

12. Be an advocate for institutional changes that will enhance the opportunities for returning women.

13. Provide a supportive atmosphere for self-exploration.

72

As institutions evaluate their re-entry programs, they should examine other colleges and universities that have developed extensive support programs for re-entry women; University of Maryland-College Park, University of Michigan, Foothill College, and DeAnza College are a few examples.

Conclusion

Evidence indicates that greater proportions of adult women are attending institutions of higher learning than ever before. Many institutions still do not provide freely supportive climates that assist re-entry women in their pursuit of a degree. These women represent a special population and are entitled to the understanding that comes from an increasingly sophisticated body of knowledge concerning their needs and the issues they face. Institutions as a whole must develop a keen awareness of the special needs of these women and develop policies and programs to assist them in their return to education. In developing these programs, institutions must be aware of the diversity that exists among returning women students and offer a variety of support services designed to meet specific needs.

The significance of higher education does not lie in the number of women attending. It is significant only when it raises the intellectual and cultural level of the whole society, when it endorses and rigorously pursues the fullest development of the intellectual, artistic, and professional aspirations of all students (Astin, 1976).

References

Astin, H. "Adult Development and Education." In H. Astin (Ed.), *Some Action of Her Own.* Lexington, Mass.: DeHeath, 1976.

Benjamin, E. *Barriers to Academic Re-Entry Women and How to Overcome Them.* Evanston, Ill.: Northwestern University, Program Women, 1979.

Brandenburg, J. B. "The Needs of Women Returning to School." *Personnel and Guidance Journal,* 1974, *53* (1), 11–18.

Chickering, A. W. *Education and Identity.* San Francisco: Jossey-Bass, 1969.

Creange, R. "Student Support Services: Re-Entry Women Need Them Too." Washington, D.C.: Association of American Colleges Project on the Status and Education of Women, 1980. (ERIC Document, ED 193980)

Deutsch, F., and Hultsch, D. F. *Adult Aging and Development: A Life-Span Perspective.* New York: McGraw-Hill, 1981.

Dunkle, M. C. "Financial Aid: Helping Re-Entry Women Pay College Costs—What Institutions Can Do to Provide Financial Resources to Women Re-Entering the Educational System." Washington, D.C.: Association of American Colleges Project on the Status of Education of Women, Department of Education, 1980. (ERIC Document, ED 193980)

Karelius-Schumacher, K. C. "Designing a Counseling Program for the Mature Woman Student." *Journal of the National Association for Women Deans, Administrators, and Counse-. lors,* 1977, *41* (1), 28–31.

Letchworth, G. E. "Women Who Return to College: An Identity-Integrity Approach." *Journal of College Student Personnel,* 1970, *11* (2), 103–106.

Maes, N. *Re-Entry: A Handbook for Adult Women Students.* Evanston, Ill.: Northwestern University, 1979.

Markus, H. *Continuing Education for Women: Factors Influencing a Return to School and School Experience.* Ann Arbor: University of Michigan, 1973. (ERIC Document, ED 028296)

Molstad, S. M. "Re-Entry Women: Extending an Invitation." *Journal of the National Association for Women Deans, Administrators, and Counselors,* 1984, *47* (2), 37–39.

Plotsky, F. A. "The Ivory Tower and Students Older than Average." *Journal of the National Association for Women Deans, Administrators, and Counselors,* 1975, *39* (1), 21–25.

Saslaw, R. W. "A New Student for the Eighties: The Mature Woman." *Educational Horizons,* 1981, *69* (1), 41–46.

Scott, N. A. *Returning Women Students: A Review of Research and Descriptive Studies.* Washington, D.C.: National Association for Women Deans, Administrators, and Counselors, 1980.

Tittle, C. K., and Denker, E. R. *Returning Women Students in Higher Education: Defining Policy Issues.* New York: Praeger, 1980.

Gay Holliday is the director of staff services at the University of Illinois-Chicago and former coordinator of educational programs and services for the Association of College Unions-International.

This chapter summarizes both the real characteristics and the stereotypes of minority women that affect the delivery of student services, and it includes recommendations for better education and assistance for these groups in their college careers.

Addressing the Special Needs of Minority Women

Carolyn R. Payton

Writing about the development of minority women is more difficult than may readily be apparent, for both what we are and the image we project may be as much the consequence of how we have been portrayed as they are a consequence of genetics, gender, and/or socialization. Historically, the male members of the predominant society — particularly the researchers, anthropologists, historians, and even fiction writers — are the ones who have etched out the parameters of our personas. The creations of these men may have been as close to or as far from reality as the fabled blind men's description of an elephant. Reality notwithstanding, the paucity of countervailing data generated by minorities themselves that have been accepted for publication has meant that the generalizations of those alien to minority women have prevailed and been accepted as accurate.

For example, black women have been presented as strong, competent, domineering, and the least "feminine" of all females. First, we may ask whether this is a true reflection of black women. Next, we may ask to what degree these traits are attributable to our West African heritage rather than the impact of slavery. Rodgers-Rose (1980) writes that the West African woman was independent, managing the market

N. J. Evans (Ed.). *Facilitating the Development of Women.* New Directions for Student Services, no. 29. San Francisco: Jossey-Bass, March 1985.

system and retaining her earnings. She did not expect her husband to bear responsibility for her. The conditions she experienced in slavery reinforced this independent life-style since there was no one else upon whom she could depend.

Since there were circumstances supporting the development of strength and self-reliance, it is not surprising that black women began to be described as matriarchs. However, slavery cut the West African ties and the Civil War dispelled the ethos of slavery. What now sustains and reinforces the mythical image of black women as having limitless resources of strength and courage? One answer may well be the lack of realistic information documenting the real life experiences of black women.

Documentation demonstrates that erosions of traditional sex roles occur. Beatrice Medicine (1980) describes the role transferences occurring among native Americans when they were forced to live on reservations. This life effectively destroyed the warrier-hunter-provider role for males, while the Indian woman was forced to negotiate with her soldier guards and government agents in ways that were far from customary for her. Additionally, the destruction of the bison, which were so fundamental to her welfare and life-style, resulted in her having to confront different work demands. Wittstock (1980) and Whiteman (1980) also described how the roles of Indian women were changed as efforts were made to "civilize" them. They were often forced to seek employment outside the home as opposed to remaining with their families in order to maintain the Indian tribal institutions of family network and bonds (Whiteman, 1980).

Additional instances of the distortion of traditional female roles by conquerors or by those who possessed the power to define women can be found in the writings on all minority women. All have been constricted by the expectations and attitudes conveyed to the public in general by predominantly male social scientists, if and when they are mentioned at all.

This chapter represents an effort to offset the balance of coverage given minority women in the typical training program of student services workers. Psychology and education curricula do not prepare these professionals adequately to address and deal effectively with the concerns of minority women. Writing this chapter provides an opportunity to contribute to the quality of education and training of student service professionals with special respect to female minority populations, with the hope that culturally sensitive models for the delivery of these services will thus be promoted.

Basic Assumptions Regarding Student Development Goals

Fenske (1980) suggests that the student services profession's acceptance of responsibility for education of the "whole" person is no longer warranted. I disagree with this position. The basic assumptions I hold with regard to the goals of student development follow:

1. I believe that the primary direct responsibility of the college or university is to provide for the intellectual growth and skill development of its student population.

2. I believe that the student services professional adheres to the premise that education of the whole person is a valid, viable, and useful concept.

3. Student services are critical components of higher education in that they increase the possibilities of students gaining the maximum from their academic experience, and this, in turn, will lead to maximum intellectual growth and skill development.

The theories undergirding student services are sound and relevant to minority populations. Applying these theories to minority women, however, has been a problem, and the specific needs of these groups are not being addressed adequately due to the lack of knowledge about these women. An overview of the critical issues affecting the development of ethnic minority women should be instructive to those who would facilitate their development.

Native American Women

Native Americans make up 9.5 percent of the general population. According to Trimble (1977), they are dispersed among no less than 250 tribal groups, each of which is a sovereign entity. Tribes are found in urban as well as rural settings. They are quite diverse culturally, ranging from matrilineal to patrilineal. It is thus erroneous to think of the native American as a monolithic individual, although native Americans share a common heritage in experiencing a variety of attempts to annihilate them as a group. This strategy for their destruction was eventually altered and replaced by a more "benign" goal of destroying the Indian culture under the guise of "civilization" and the "melting pot" philosophy.

Partly as a consequence of adaptation to the dominant culture and as a direct result of economic pressures, increasing numbers of native American women are seeking the chance to avail themselves of legitimate postsecondary school education. One could substitute the term "institutionalized" for "legitimate," but, in either case, the term has been used deliberately to indicate that native American women have neither lacked education nor have they devalued education. All these tribal cultures, through hundreds of years, have developed systematic models for transmitting to each succeeding generation the expected behavior for adults (Attneave and Dill, 1980). Native Americans have possessed this ability to an amazing extent, despite many tribes' lack of a written language. Education in a formal sense was introduced to the native Americans by the missionaries and boarding schools run by the Bureau of Indian Affairs agents. Readings from this period show that the focus of such education was the indoctrination of the native American with the Protestant work ethic. Although there was great concern for the superficial replication of the "civilized" person (for example, in haircuts, new clothes, and the "squeaky clean" look), there seems to have been little attention or concern paid to the enhancement of the native American's cognitive development.

Marlene Echohawk (1979) depicts the impact of early efforts to "educate" native American children most succinctly:

> Even the most well-intentioned efforts, for example, to "facilitate" acculturation by means of boarding schools for children have in effect disrupted the Indian community, altered the extended family structure, changed traditional family networks, created conflicts in life goals, and so forth. The result of these varied intrusions include widespread depression, negative self-image, and internal and external conflicts all reflected in high suicides, accidental death rates, and a high incidence of alcoholism [pp. 964–965].

In spite of this less than salubrious introduction to westernized eduation, many native Americans, including women, have come to believe that survival is possible only through education. Education has come to be viewed as a means of improving their economic status as well as bettering the lot of their families and communities.

To many native American women, the pursuit of educational degrees or professional training is still deemed potentially disruptive of traditional life-styles. The woman who treasures the generations-old value of her role as the primary caretaker of children and supporter of her mate can be expected to experience conflict when confronted with the option of a college education. The native American woman who holds to the tradition that family and tribal bonds are of the highest priority may easily question the relevance of a higher education to her life's goals and values.

The native American woman seen on our campuses has obviously made a step toward resolving the contradictory forces that rule the lives of contemporary native Americans — their traditional life-style versus assimilation into the wider culture. But do not conclude from her presence that she has abandoned her Indianness, as she may well be a part-time native American (Krutz, 1973). A part-time native American is one who understands some of the so-called advantages accrued from living in the dominant society — such advantages as living in a home with modern appliances, owning a car, and having a wide range of recreational and leisure time opportunities — yet is a person who resists becoming digested into the mainstream of white society.

So our native American woman may well have decided to retain her ethnic identity while reaping the benefits of higher education. The price she pays for this duality has been captured in the writings of Linda Edgewater (1981), a Navajo graduate student. She reports that Navajos learn that time is infinite, collaborative and cooperative behavior is prized, submissiveness and humbleness are rewarded, and working to satisfy present needs and to be in harmony with nature is vital. This belief system clashes with the qualities emphasized in Anglo schools, where it is expected that deadlines should be met, aggressive and competitive behaviors are positively rewarded, future gratification is extolled, and the mastery of nature is assumed. Should the student accept the Anglo's values in place of her traditional ones, disharmony is caused and physical and mental illness may be the result. Yet, if she fails to adopt the qualities most closely associated with academic achievement, her educational progress will be imperiled. To get out of this dilemma, the native American women may choose to become a part-time native American.

A second view of the native American female student can be garnered from the writing of Kidwell (1980). From her studies, a general profile can be drawn of the native American woman college student:

> She is interested in a career, probably one in a social-service-related field, intends to work after graduation, is somewhat older than the typical student entering college directly out of high school, is given as much or more encouragement by her family to go to college as her male relatives, and, if she feels discriminated against herself, attributes it more to racism than to sexism [p. 107].

Kidwell also reports there is some evidence that native American women incur condescension and disapproving attitudes from native American males if and when they seek college education. We may assume that such attitudes probably stem from the male's acceptance of the traditional view that a woman's place is in the home, or, at the very least, that she should not compete with him for jobs.

Asian-American Pacific Islanders

The reader is again cautioned that, while the term Asian-American Pacific islanders may evoke an image of a neat grouping of homogeneous individuals, such a conclusion is in great error. Cordova (1980) states that the Asian group is composed of Japanese, Chinese, Filipinos, Koreans, Vietnamese, Cambodians, Thais, and East Indians. The term also encompasses people from the Pacific islands of Samoa, Guam, Hawaii, and Tonga. Given the diversity of home of origin, the members of this group may be differentiated by such other dimensions as: area of residence in the United States, socioeconomic status, degree of acculturation, economic status, and financial standing. It should be obvious that the reader must be judicious and discerning in generalizing about Asian-American women, as this group is anything but homogeneous.

The one thing that these women all do share is the experience of varying degrees of discrimination, racism, and prejudice. The Chinese and Japanese immigrated to the United States in the 1840s and 1890s, respectively. Each was confronted with an aggressive and persistent hostility culminating in the passage of various legislation designed to legalize the differential treatment to which they were subjected. Sue (1981) highlights the massive discrimination that Asians faced: "Denied the rights of citizenship, denied ownership of land, assaulted, murdered, and placed in concentration camps during World War II, Asians in America have at one time or another been subjected to the most appalling forms of discrimination ever perpetrated against any immigrant group" (p. 115).

In spite of this inauspicious reception in the United States, Asian-Americans have in recent years been awarded the title of "model minority." They have been held up to other Americans as minorities who have "made it." Definitions of success are given as:

- A greater percentage of Asian females completing college than for all U.S. females
- Asian-Americans' income exceeding the national median
- A reduction of the social distance between Asians and whites as evidenced by the 50 percent incidence of interracial marriages
- Low official rates of juvenile delinquency

- Low rates of psychiatric contact and hospitalization
- Low rates of divorce.

In reviewing these data, we can see how the conclusion was reached that all is well with the Asian-American; however, Hirata (1980) dispels this notion of success with regard to women. She points out that the improvement of Asian-American women's status, so frequently cited in the literature, is merely an illusion, and that there is little relationship between level of education and occupation and income of Asian women. True-Homma (1980), in a study of Bay Area Asians, also documents the disparity between educational achievement and earned income of Asian women.

Derald Sue (1981) vehemently argues against the notion of Asians as model citizens and minorities. He advises a closer look behind the tourist attractions of Chinatown(s), Manilatown(s), and Japantown(s) in our major cities to see the prevalent unemployment, poverty, health problems, and crime.

Asian-American women, as is true for native American women, may be viewed from the perspective of their adherence to traditional cultural beliefs versus their adoption of contemporary life-styles. Historically, the Asian woman has been reared within a patriarchal structure in which numerous constraints were placed upon women (True-Homma, 1980). Being a female was considered highly undesirable, so she was relegated to an inferior status. Her destiny was to serve her family until she married, then to bear children, serving her husband and sons until the latter married, and preserving family unity until death.

Overlaying her sense of inferiority and worthlessness were general Asian cultural values identified by Sue (1973): "Traditional Asian values emphasize reserve and formality in interpersonal relations, restraint and inhibition of strong feelings, obedience to authority, obligations to the family, high academic and occupational achievement, and use of shame and guilt to control behavior" (p. 141).

Sue also concluded, based on his study of Japanese and Chinese students at the University of California at Berkeley, that Asian-Americans of both sexes (1) tend to evaluate ideas on the basis of their immediate practical application and avoid an abstract, reflective, theoretical orientation; (2) are less tolerant of ambiguity; (3) are less autonomous and independent from parental control and authority figures; and (4) are more obedient, conservative, conforming, and inhibited.

Based on the data reported in the preceding discussion, we can draw a profile of the Asian-American female college student. She is highly motivated to achieve and is inclined toward business occupations, applied technical fields, and biological or physical sciences. These are probably her interests because these areas are most likely to shelter her from close, interpersonal relationships and will limit her involvement with people. The foregoing areas also tend to be more exact and thus could spare the Asian-American woman the discomfort she might feel if she had to deal with more abstract material. She is not prone to maintaining ethnic purity as would seem to be true for native American women, and she will adopt those facets of Western culture that she sees as functional and reject those that do not serve her purposes. Assimilation is a more viable option for her than it would seem to be for native American women.

Hispanic American Women

In this section, we are again compelled to use a generic label that reflects little of the enormous complexities and diversities of the population so entitled. The term "Hispanic" refers to all Spanish-speaking or Spanish-surnamed people who reside in the United States or Puerto Rico. Mexican Americans, Cuban Americans, and Puerto Ricans are the major Hispanic groups. According to Bernal and others (1983), Puerto Ricans and Cubans on the East Coast prefer to be identified as Hispanics, while on the West Coast the preference is for the term "Latino." Mexican Americans or persons of Mexican heritage are usually referred to as Chicano.

The complexity and diversity of this group are also supported by a review of their history (Sue, 1981; Jimenez-Vasquez, 1980; Bernal and others, 1983; Smith, 1984). By virtue of the Mexican-American War, which ended with the signing of the Treaty of Guadalupe Hidalgo in 1848, all Mexicans living in what is now New Mexico, Arizona, and California immediately became "hyphenated Americans." Because of such apparent differences as skin color and language, the newly incorporated citizens of the United States became isolated and thus retained their culture relatively intact. Additionally, the population of Mexican Americans was increased by the migrations of Mexicans to the southwestern United States following the 1910 Mexican Revolution.

Puerto Ricans' connection with the United States is also unique. Puerto Rico was invaded by the United States during the Spanish-American War and has never become independent. Like American blacks, Puerto Ricans did not elect to become citizens but became so when Spain ceded their island to the U.S. The United States then granted them American citizenship in 1917. A mass migration of Puerto

Ricans to the States occurred during World War II in response to the availability of jobs on the mainland, but for the most part the migrants were from rural areas of the island with little facility in English and little more than an elementary school education.

Mass migration from Cuba to the States took place after the 1959 Cuban Revolution. These new citizens were typically the wealthy of the island. The second large migration took place after the Bay of Pigs invasion in 1961, but this time the migrants were from the professional and highly skilled group of white-collar workers. More recent migrants have consisted primarily of the lower-middle and lower classes — that is, blue-collar workers and laborers.

This brief history of the arrival of the major Hispanic groups in the U.S. should serve to illustrate the variations found among them. Further, Puerto Ricans and Cubans share a common ancestry of black Moors and Africans, and all three groups additionally have Indian forebears.

Hispanic women's cultural group membership can best be conceptualized on a continuum (Sue, 1981); on one end of the continuum women can be found who hold total commitment to the Anglo culture, while at the other end are found women who are equally as committed to the Hispanic culture. Probably most of the women on our campuses from this group are in between and are both bicultural and bilingual. Ruiz (1981) points out that, for many Hispanics, situations may determine the cultural identity they assume. A woman, for example, is likely to be very Anglo at school and very Hispanic when at home or among family members.

One general cultural value that is attributed to Hispanics by all writers is the importance of the family. The family unit is viewed as the single most important element in Hispanic culture, including not only the immediate blood relatives, their spouses, and children, but also the extended family — aunts, uncles, cousins, nephews, and nieces.

A second predominant Hispanic cultural theme is that of the assumed prevalence of *machismo*. Ruiz (1981) asserts that non-Hispanics mistakenly identify "macho" as referring to a male who is physically aggressive, sexually promiscuous, and who dominates his woman totally and drinks excessively. Hispanics view "macho" as a male who has a great sense of responsibility for all members of his family, who sees himself as the economic provider of the family, and who is the main authority for family decisions. He is the protector. The wife's role is to be completely supportive of her husband, and for some women this lack of role confusion leads to a clearer self-concept and thus to a healthier personality.

Collado-Herrell and Herrell (1979) looked at Hispanic culture by comparing Puerto Rican women with their U.S. counterparts and developed this list of differences. Puerto Rican women are: (1) more attached to their nuclear and extended families; (2) more subservient to their husbands; (3) more responsible for the minute-to-minute behavior of their children; and (4) more dependent on parents and husbands.

It is quite difficult to generate a profile of the Hispanic college female because of the differences found among the major groups. Arce (Arce and others, 1983) states that Hispanics as a group defy categorization because of heterogeneity not only in national origin but in customs and level of acculturation.

The Black American Female

The first Africans arrived in American in 1619, and in 1661 Virginia passed legislation enslaving persons of African heritage for life. Perkins (1983) and Smith (1984) present a most enlightening social and historical overview of the black woman in America. Since women's education during the nineteenth century was designed to reinforce the notion that females were primarily the helpmates of their spouses and caretakers of the children, women's training focused on the domestic arts, needlework, music, painting, and so forth. Such education, however, was intended only for middle- and upper-class white women. Black women, slaves or not, were considered as less than human and were not held to the preceding objectives, which defined "pure womanhood."

Blacks were more concerned with the improvement of the race than they were with maintaining the "purity of womanhood." Thus, they were more prone to establish coeducational schools with similar curricula for both sexes. Oberlin became the first institution of higher education to open its doors to both women and blacks in 1833. The first black woman to earn a college degree in the United States graduated from this college in 1862. After the Civil War, many schools for blacks were established with the help of Northern missionaries and white women from New England who came to the South to teach.

The egalitarian attitudes of black men seem to have faded away with the Emancipation Proclamation. At the primary school level, black males and females were in approximately equal proportions, but black men far outnumbered black women in higher education. Black women who did manage to go to college were largely trained to become elementary and secondary school teachers, and their male counterparts were not so constrained. Perkins (1983) writes that, as black men wanted to achieve position and education similar to white men, many internalized the prevailing notion of white males that women are inferior and thus subordinate. So were sown the seeds of the double oppression — sexism and racism — borne by black women in the United States.

A profile of the black college woman can be generated from the annual data collection on college students conducted by the American Council on Education using the Student Information Form (Astin and others, 1983). The most recent available data come from respondents in the entering class of 1983. The average black college woman has never married, is eighteen years old, and was a 1982 high school graduate. The majority of black women ranked at about the academic median in their high school class, and they were less tied than their predecessors to traditional female occupations, such as nursing, teaching, and social work, and were more interested in business and engineering as probable majors. The black female's educational aspirations equaled those of the black male student in that she expected to earn a degree in medicine or dentistry or a Ph.D. or Ed.D. degree as often as black males. As many as one-third expected to earn at least a master's degree. How the black woman ended up as a person seemed to depend upon whether she enrolled in a predominantly white or a predominantly black college.

Fleming (1983) conducted a study in which she compared a sample of freshmen and seniors drawn from mostly black and mostly white colleges in order to infer the impact of each. She found that the adverse conditions under which black women lived in primarily white colleges were more likely to encourage self-reliance and assertiveness, characteristics associated with the matriarch image commonly used to describe black women. The supportive conditions of the predominantly black schools were more likely to encourage social passivity or the image of the "victim," another common descriptor used for black women.

Just as this study suggests that the college environment can influence the development of black women, the same is doubtless true for all ethnic minority women. What can student services personnel do to make the college experience a positive one for these women?

Implications

The most succinct summary of the presentation here on minority women is that they are different. Yet they, too, deserve the opportunity to develop optimally through participating in the educational process offered by colleges and universities. Student services personnel have a responsibility to recruit, admit, and provide support services for this population. They must also be concerned about providing services that aim at the retention of these students.

According to the latest census data, in the fall 1982 semester a total of 599,287 ethnic minority women were enrolled as full-time or part-time students in 1,959 institutions of higher education granting at least a bachelor's degree. That is a sizable number of women. When graduation statistics are consulted, it becomes apparent that the percent of minority women completing a college education is less than might be expected. For example, minority women comprise 16.7 percent of the total number of enrolled students, but only 13.7 percent of the students receiving bachelor's degrees (U.S. Department of Education, 1983). What steps might be taken to increase the proportion finishing their career in higher education?

Student services personnel from the admissions officer to the veterans affairs officer must be imbued with the urgency of proffering appropriate services to this population. "Higher education" means giving opportunities to minority women while at the same time giving them chances to become upwardly mobile, so that they will not be represented so disproportionately in low-paying jobs. Their spouses do not fare much better, unfortunately. Unlike many majority women, minorities are not in college largely to find husbands, for they enroll and attend to gain the skills that will allow them to find secure employment, enabling them to live in a more comfortable manner and raise their families accordingly. Frequently, they have delayed entering the work force because of the time that it takes to complete their education, and this entails a considerable sacrifice on the part of their families, who must do without the additional paycheck but who must still continue to contribute to the educational expense.

The first priority for colleges and universities is to recruit minority women. This means going where the minorities live. In order to attract these people, recruiters must venture into inner cities, reservations, or other areas with high concentrations of minority families. Using minority alumnae when possible, recruiters have proved to be quite successful in bringing about the enrollment of additional minority women.

Until there is a truly culture-free test for assessing either intelligence or academic achievement, Scholastic Aptitude Test (SAT) and American College Test (ACT) scores will continue to underestimate the abilities of most minorities. The predictive validities of these tests may be especially low when administered to those whose native language is other than English, since it has been demonstrated that these groups are particularly handicapped by these instruments. The admissions office must be alert to other indexes besides test scores that can be used to predict collegiate success and achievement. If the institution administers the tests, pains should be taken to include minorities among the test givers and assistants, since the addition of these people may render the testing situation less threatening and lower the level of anxiety.

Many minorities do not remain in college or even seek admission due to the lack of funds. We should encourage increases in scholarships, fellowships, and other forms of financial aid. Next, the financial aid office must take steps to get the necessary information about available assistance programs out to minorities. According to an article in *The Chronicle of Higher Education* ("Inadequate Information," 1984), many needy students have little or no access to data concerning financial aid. This lack of knowledge may have contributed to the lack of growth in the number of minority students who have been enrolled over the past decade.

One sure way of minimizing the feelings of alienation so often reported by minority students is to increase their numbers in the campus environment. Aggressive and innovative efforts must be undertaken to enlist minority women faculty and administrators as well as students. At present a plateau in these groups has been reached. The news media (Mackay-Smith, 1984; "Minorities Seen Making No Gain," 1984) report an underrepresentation of minorities as faculty and as administrators. Few gains can be expected unless the potential pool of minority professionals increases, which can only happen by increasing the minority student population as a whole. Student services personnel have the talent needed to design and conduct workshops for those individuals responsible for recruiting minorities, and they should develop and implement these at every opportunity.

Career planning offices should construct programs aimed at reaching minority women students early in their college years. These students need information about accessing nontraditional fields as majors and about job possibilities within these fields. Remember that minority students may not have been exposed to role models performing a variety of occupational duties. Numerous career options may simply not have occurred to these women.

Counselors must be encouraged to keep abreast of what little literature there is on ethnic minority women and adopt appropriate treatment or intervention models. Whenever possible, the counseling staff should reflect the cultural and ethnic diversity of our society, but if this is not possible, the employer of future staff must examine resumés and transcripts of applicants for evidence of relevant experiences and training in working with the culturally different. Workshops should be offered to university officials who might have contact with minority students in order to increase these administrators' cultural sensitivities.

A major concern reported by minority women enrolled at predominantly white institutions is the lack of male companionship. Black women, in particular, find that black men avail themselves of the opportunity and willingness of white coeds to date. Black women are not as apt to date white men due to memory traces of their ancestors' subjugation and sexual exploitation by white males. Others do not mix socially with white men because of their awareness of the threat this portends to black men, and still others feel white men appear to be less receptive to them as women, especially when compared with the eagerness with which they feel white women respond to black men. Whatever the reason, the limited opportunities for male-female interaction during this phase of minority women's lives should be attended to by student services personnel. Minority women's support groups should be conducted at least to give these women an avenue for exploring their feelings and expressing their emotions.

A review of the literature on minority women makes it painfully obvious that, as a result of both historical and social factors, these populations do indeed have special needs. Even more important is the realization that these special needs are no more than a reflection of the deficits in our society. Were it not for prejudice and discrimination, elementary and secondary education would have more adequately equipped minority women to handle the demands of higher education. Were it not for the oppression and rejection experienced by virtue of racism and sexism, these women would be freer to strive for optimal development. Were it not for intolerance, these women could more readily capitalize on their natural strengths and become more fully self-actualized. Where there is prejudice and intolerance, minority women are inevitably the recipients. Student services personnel must do what they can to allow these women to achieve their human right to self-determination.

References

Arce, A., Diaz, M., Galbis, R., and Garcia, R. "Development of Hispanic Curricula in Psychiatric Residency Programs." In J. C. Chunn II, P. J. Dunston, and F. Ross-Sheriff (Eds.), *Mental Health and People of Color: Curriculum Development and Change.* Washington, D.C.: Howard University Press, 1983.

Astin, A. W., and others. *The American Freshman: National Norms for Fall 1983.* Los Angeles: Cooperative Institutional Reserach Program, Graduate School of Education, University of California, 1983.

Attneave, C. L., and Dill, A. "Indian Boarding Schools and Indian Women: Blessing or Curse?" In *Conference on the Educational and Occupational Needs of American Indian Women.* Washington, D.C.: U.S. Department of Education, National Institute of Education, 1980.

Bernal, G., Bernal, M. E., Martinez, A. C., Olmedo, E. L., and Santiseban, D. "Hispanic Mental Health Curriculum for Psychology." In J. C. Chunn II, P. J. Dunston, and R. Ross-Sheriff (Eds.), *Mental Health and People of Color: Curriculum Development and Change.* Washington, D.C.: Howard University Press, 1983.

Collado-Herrell, L., and Herrell, J. "The Puerto Rican Woman: Her Role in Substance Abuse." In *Proceedings of Forum on Substance Abuse: Prevention of, by, and for Bicultural Women.* Washington, D.C.: National Institute of Drug Abuse, 1979.

Cordova, D. L. "Education Alternatives for Asian-Pacific Women." In *Conference on the Educational and Occupational Needs of Asian-Pacific-American Women.* Washington, D.C.: U.S. Department of Education, National Institute of Education, 1980.

Echohawk, M. "Views of Chemical Substance Abuse by American Indian Women." In *Proceedings of Forum on Substance Abuse: Prevention of, by, and for Bicultural Women.* Washington, D.C.: National Institute of Drug Abuse, 1979.

Edgewater, L. "Stress and Navajo University Students." *Journal of American Indian Education,* 1981, *20* (3), 25–31.

Fenske, R. H. "Current Trends." In U. Delworth, G. R. Hanson, and Associates (Eds.), *Student Services: A Handbook for the Profession.* San Francisco: Jossey-Bass, 1980.

Fleming, J. "Black Women in Black and White College Environments: The Making of a Matriarch." *Journal of Social Issues,* 1983, *39* (3), 41–54.

Hirata, L. C. "Social Mobility of Asian Women in America: A Critical Review." In *Conference on the Educational and Occupational Needs of Asian-Pacific-American Women.* Washington, D.C.: U.S. Department of Education, National Institute of Education, 1980.

"Inadequate Information on Financial Aid Blamed for Slow Growth of Minority School Enrollment." *Chronicle of Higher Education,* April 18, 1984, pp. 19, 21.

Jimenez-Vasquez, R. "Social Issues Confronting Hispanic American Women." In *Conference on the Educational and Occupational Needs of Hispanic Women.* Washington, D.C.: U.S. Department of Education, National Institute of Education, 1980.

Kidwell, C. S. "The Status of American Indian Women in Higher Education." In *Conference on the Educational and Occupational Needs of American Indian Women.* Washington, D.C.: U.S. Department of Education, National Institute of Education, 1980.

Krutz, G. "Compartmentalization as a Factor in Urban Adjustment: The Kiowa Case." In J. O. Waddell and O. M. Watson (Eds.), *American Indian Urbanization.* Monograph Series No. 4. West Lafayette, Ind.: Purdue Research Foundation, 1973.

Mackay-Smith, A. "Large Shortage of Black Professors in Higher Education Grows Worse." *Wall Street Journal,* June 12, 1984, p. 37.

Medicine, B. "The Interaction of Culture and Sex Roles in the Schools." In *Conference on the Educational and Occupational Needs of American Indian Women.* Washington, D.C.: U.S. Department of Education, National Institute of Education, 1980.

"Minorities Seen Making No Gain in Campus Jobs." *Chronicle of Higher Education,* June 13, 1984, pp. 1, 20.

Perkins, L. "The Impact of the 'Cult of True Womanhood' on the Education of Black Women." *Journal of Social Issues,* 1983, *39* (3), 17–28.

Rodgers-Rose, L. F. *The Black Woman.* Beverly Hills, Calif.: Sage, 1980.

Ruiz, R. A. "Cultural and Historical Perspective in Counseling Hispanics." In D. W. Sue (Ed.), *Counseling the Culturally Different: Theory and Practice.* New York: Wiley, 1981.

Smith, P. *The Rise of Industrial America.* New York: McGraw-Hill, 1984.

Sue, D. W. "Ethnic Identity: The Impact of Two Cultures on the Psychological Development of Asians in America." In S. Sue and N. Wagner (Eds.), *Asian-Americans' Psychological Perspectives.* Palo Alto, Calif.: Science & Behavior Books, 1973.

Sue, D. W. *Counseling the Culturally Different: Theory and Practice.* New York: Wiley, 1981.

Trimble, J. E. "The Sojourner in the American Indian Community: Methodological Issues and Concerns." *Journal of Social Issues,* 1977, *33* (4), 159–174.

True-Homma, R. "Mental Health Issues Among Asian-American Women." In *Conference on the Educational and Occupational Needs of Asian-Pacific-American Women.* Washington, D.C.: U.S. Department of Education, National Institute of Education, 1980.

U.S. Department of Education. *Data on Earned Degrees Conferred by Institutions of Higher Education by Race, Ethnicity, and Sex for Academic Year 1980–81.* Washington, D.C.: U.S. Department of Education, Office of Civil Rights, 1983.

Whiteman, H. "Insignificance of Humanity: 'Man Is Tampering with the Moon and the Stars.'" In *Conference on the Educational and Occupational Needs of American Indian Women.* Washington, D.C.: U.S. Department of Education, National Institute of Education, 1980.

Wittstock, L. W. "Native American Women: Twilight of a Long Maidenhood." In B. Lindsey (Ed.), *Comparative Perspectives of Third-World Women.* New York: Praeger, 1980.

Carolyn R. Payton is dean for counseling and career development at Howard University, Washington, D.C. Prior to holding this position, she was appointed by President Carter to serve as director of the U.S. Peace Corps, the first woman and black leader of the organization.

Implementation of developmental programming for women
requires administrative commitment and a solid research base.

Administrative Challenges and Future Directions

Susan R. Komives
Nancy J. Evans

A feminist philosophy is essential to counsel, teach, and program effectively for women students. A frequent flaw of coed schools and other nonfeminist institutions is to assume that women are doing well developmentally because they adjust to the male norm. Commenting on the wave of coeducation that swept many prestigious men's institutions, Debra Herman (1980) remarks that "coeducation proceeded on the theory that access alone was sufficient, that all that needed to be done was to plug women into institutions and programs of study once open to men only. . . requiring few more substantial changes than new lettering on some bathroom doors" (p. 156).

Most coeducational campuses and many women's institutions have never examined the assumptions behind the nature of men's or women's learning either inside or outside the classroom. Most campuses follow the format of higher education passed down through centuries of academia. This format may not be the most growth producing for many men students, let alone the increasing number of women students enrolled on our campuses.

N. J. Evans (Ed.). *Facilitating the Development of Women.* New Directions
for Student Services, no. 29. San Francisco: Jossey-Bass, March 1985.

Jesse Bernard (1981) asserts that "academic learning is incomplete, biased, parochial. It has little to say about women and the world of women" (p. 271). Whether in women's studies courses or mainstreamed into departmental curriculum, inclusion of the new scholarship on women offers "more women a new intellectual grasp on their lives, new understanding of our history, a fresh vision of the human experience, and also a critical basis for evaluating what they hear and read in other courses, and in the society at large" (Rich, 1979, p. 233).

When examining how the assumptions behind learning affect women, many faculty and administrators do not even know the questions to ask. At a conference celebrating 150 years of women's education at Stephens College, Elizabeth Minnich (1984) suggested applying two simple, generic questions — (1) how does this apply to women, and (2) was it supposed to — to the subject matter of any program, book, research study, or theory in order to focus analysis on the right issues affecting women.

No area of scholarship is immune from the exclusion of gender differences. In an extensive review of the literature, Follett and others (1982) found that gender was infrequently a variable studied by researchers looking at the college students' experience. They note that "researchers have not been sensitive to the possibility that the college environment may be different for women than for men and that sex-role socialization may generate different responses by women as compared to men in that environment" (p. 525). Their study of 238 veterinary medicine students found significant sex differences in five areas: "peer relationships, gender role expectations, perceived sex discrimination in the college (including offensive comments by faculty), and attitudes on self-disclosure and general competitiveness" (p. 526).

In a similar study, sociologists Bolton and Kammeyer (1967) actually found "larger differences between the sexes than between their four primary classifications; they consequently expanded the number of their classifications to eight to reflect gender differences. Although those sociologists used as a basis of their typology students' level of involvement with the college, another effective approach would be to use sex or sex-role orientation as the basis for defining a subculture" (Follett and others, 1982, p. 530).

In a study examining the relationship between satisfaction and performance in college, Bean and Bradley (1984) found significant differences between men and women in the importance attached to various aspects of the college experience. Satisfaction with the college environment was significantly related to grade point average (GPA) for women but not for men. They report that "Women seem to respond positively to the nurturance of the environment. That is, if staff, faculty, and other students provide an environment in which the woman feels she belongs and has friends who support her, she is more likely to perform well academically" (p. 23).

Clearly the college environment is perceived differently by the men and women who study, learn, and live there. Campus educators must examine the nature of the college experience to increase the growth potential for women (and other minorities) whose experience is different from the assumptions of the predominant white male norm. Campus programming must directly and indirectly address women's needs.

This chapter will discuss barriers to effective programming for women and suggest ways in which such programming can be encouraged. An action agenda deserving of administrative support will be presented. Finally, the application of feminist principles to student affairs divisions will be discussed, and suggestions for future research related to women's development will be provided.

Barriers to Programming for Women

We must believe that campuses are staffed by sensitive administrators and faculty who sincerely want students to learn and grow. While there are always a few genuinely unfeeling people, most campus staff intend to be caring and effective. Their ineffectiveness in response to women students' needs may be attributed to lack of understanding of issues, personal and professional burnout, or unclear institutional goals. Unfortunately, there continue to be too many cases of actual sexism — faculty and administrators who judge women and their issues to be unimportant or insignificant.

Whether programming is student initiated or staff designed, there are numerous institutional barriers and personal myths to overcome to attain any measure of success. Programmers would do well to think through these messages often heard from unenlightened administrators and faculty:

- The program will be too politically sensitive or controversial (for example, programs addressing lesbian issues, choice/right-to-life issues, rape, or women's role in the church), and without doubt, the people of the state, or our alumni, would have a fit.
- If we do special programming for one group, we'll have to do it for all the other special interest groups, too.
- That incident was no big deal; after all, "boys will be boys."
- Rape (or sexual harassment, or sexism) is not that big a problem here.

- This subject is too personal; it is not scholarly and certainly is not the role of the college.
- That subject is in someone else's area — I agree it's a good idea — but it is not my responsibility (and I do not want to be labeled as a radical).
- We do not want to attract that kind of student.

In addition, programmers must be keenly aware of the messages from their intended market — students. There are few problems attracting the active and aware woman student. The messages from the unenlightened woman who remains confused by the ideologies involved must be heard:

- I'm not one of those radical feminists. I like men.
- I'm not a feminist, but . . .
- I'm interested, but if I attend that program everyone will think I am a lesbian.
- That could never happen to me or anyone I know. They're making a big deal over nothing. I've never experienced discrimination (or harassment).
- That's probably a dumb program — must not be any good if it's just for women — it must be diluted.

These insidious messages create barriers to effective programming. Sensitive administrators, faculty, and student leaders should assess the fears and reasons behind the attitudes of those people they need to persuade (whether influencers of change or the intended audience of the program) by keeping these messages in mind. These attitudes are difficult to change. The first step is to raise the awareness of the special needs of women among those perpetuating institutional barriers or holding personal misconceptions. The next steps will involve changing their behaviors to allow women's programming, and finally, changing their attitudes so that they provide actual support for that programming.

Programming for Women: Student and Staff Initiatives

The programming that exists on campuses is spawned by several motivations. James Hurst (1978) observes that most student affairs programming is influenced by three major determinants: (1) the "interest and/or orientation of the staff members comprising the student affairs division" (p. 113), (2) responses to student initiatives — their demands and requests, and (3) "political considerations and expediency" (p. 114). Clearly, one significant change strategy that student affairs staff can implement will be to hire staff already sensitive to women's issues or to develop staff awareness among those already employed.

Much campus programming is accomplished through special interest groups. Even on large campuses, some women's groups comprise fewer than a dozen devoted women. Their programming, however, reaches many, and awareness of their existence spreads to thousands. The 1978 Carnegie Surveys (Johnson, 1979) found a 21 percent increase in the number of women's groups from 1969 to 1978. In 1969, 27 percent of the institutions surveyed had a women's group while 48 percent of the institutions had such groups in 1978 (Levine, 1980, p. 37). It would seem that the re-emergence of the women's movement in the early seventies had a direct effect on this large increase in women's groups. Levine observes that all self-interest associations such as women's groups "are fragile and subject to phoenix-like appearances and disappearances with changes in leadership.... Splitting is also a problem... encouraging the formation of smaller and smaller groups" (pp. 37–38).

Levine classified activities of special interest groups into four main categories: "service, political action, education and consciousness raising, and entertainment" (p. 38). Levine notes that special interest groups have had higher visibility and generally higher levels of financing than the size of membership might normally indicate. Student government associations tend to grant substantial budgets to special interest groups that represent minority populations such as blacks and women. Levine's study of twenty-six colleges found that:

> Though quite a few women's groups are inactive, student government officials and newspaper editors praise many for their political sophistication and easy access to institutional administrators. Some are described as moribund or only "a place to go and gripe" while others are credited with substantive accomplishments, such as making a campus more aware of sexism, forcing an institution to upgrade affirmative action, stopping a fraternity pornographic film festival and wet T-shirt contest, and getting an on-campus nurse practitioner hired (p. 39).

Responsibility for Action

Too much campus programming focuses on action taken after an act of intolerance or precipitated by the political action of special interest groups. Campus administrators and faculty leaders, as educators and as employees, have a fiduciary responsibility to be proactive and not merely reactive in programming for women's needs.

Knowing what we now do about student development in general and the development of women in particular, professionals in student affairs must lead campuses in intentional interventions to educate women and men students about women's experience. Interventions must address inequities, injustices, and insensitivities that inhibit the quality of student life for women students. Buoyed by professional ethics statements, Title IX legislation, and institutional policies, the support for action exists "on paper"; our challenge is to turn that support into reality instead of lip service.

An Action Agenda

Identifying the monumental agenda implicit in each chapter of this book would take volumes. Each campus and each reader could add to the issues raised and the action needed.

The following paragraphs describe areas for action that might start the agenda-building process needed on each campus to improve the quality of experience for women students:

1. Each campus must *create a commitment to common values.* Our campuses must acknowledge that we are enriched by our diversity. We must secure recognition from senior administrators, faculty leaders, and student leaders that the development of students is an essential mission of the institution and that women students have a sufficiently unique personal and campus experience to warrant special programming. If the mission of student development is not compatible with institutional purposes, then the commitment needed must at least be to implement a nonsexist environment.

2. We must implement our values by ensuring that campuses *develop and disseminate strong institutional statements, policies, and practices on affirmative action and against any form of sexism including sexual harassment.* These goals might be accomplished by: (a) creating an awareness and support among feminist men and women who serve as role models to students; (b) committing to act when intolerable acts occur (implementing clear values and establishing processes for review); (c) validating both lesbian and heterosexual life-styles (perhaps by creating an awareness of the American Psychological Association statement on homosexuality); and (d) developing policies of nonsexist advertising in institutional and student publications.

3. Student affairs administrators must *maintain an information flow on the development of women* to key administrators and faculty. Awareness is raised when people are reminded through research reports and information memos that sift through an in-basket even if not thoroughly read. Expectations are created that at least some think it is important that this information be known. This information should include:

(a) how women's development differs from that of men; (b) differences among women (even the "nontraditional" woman comes in many forms from traditional to transitional to nontraditional); (c) support on the growing awareness of men's development; and (d) some basics of student development theory.

4. Create an awareness to *appoint women students to significant leadership roles*. Leadership roles are a source of experiential learning for students and provide an important perspective for the institution. They must be open to women students. Campuses must go one step further and implement a system to develop women leaders. In addition, both men and women campus leaders should make a commitment to mentor women students.

5. Student affairs staff must *design intentional interventions that turn theory into practice*. Knowledge about women's development, such as that presented in Chapters Two and Three of this sourcebook, must be incorporated into such areas as career counseling, life planning, advising, and course design. Theories of cognitive development provide a guide for structuring interventions while life-span theories guide us in determining issues that must be addressed.

6. Each institution must *examine institutional practices that block women's educational advancement* and must initiate needed changes. This might include the need to modify rigid load requirements that mandate full-time enrollment (in law schools, for example), an impossibility for many mothers and some men as well. It might also indicate a need to work with student honor societies that typically tap only males or more highly reward those meeting criteria based on predominantly male accomplishments.

7. As suggested in Chapters Four, Five, and Six, each campus should *create multiple opportunities for support groups* and other networks for women to connect with each other to share their common experience and find personal and political power through this support. Academic departments, sororities, women's centers, floors in residence halls, or apartment complexes provide opportunities for the development of such groups.

8. Action plans must *tap students' readiness to grow*. Programming must go where women students are. Programming must be offered in sororities, daycare centers, residence halls, commuter lounges, and in other identity bases. We must work with women in comfortable settings where they have the support to handle the challenges posed by the content of these programs.

9. As Evans, Bourassa, and Woolbright note in Chapter Four, we must acknowledge that we have a responsibility to *teach men students*

about women and, conversely, teach women about men. In addition to learning the many facets of women's experience, men must understand the phenomena of date rape and abuse as well as sex-role stereotypes. Men must learn to identify how men view women and how those views shape their behavior at work, in their families, and in relationships. Men have a lot to gain: One glorious consequence of the women's movement is the impetus for liberating men, perhaps the subject for another book.

10. Students must *be given the room to grow* and learn without rancor. Campus environments must rediscover ways for the unenlightened to ask questions and explore feminist issues without fear of being labeled sexist for not already knowing these issues.

11. As discussed in Chapters Two and Three, it is imperative that we *create an awareness among all student life staff about issues in women's development.* Just as all staff must know some basics about our profession, we must all possess some basic understanding (like the concepts presented in this book) to lead faculty, students, and others in the college community to successful women's programming. Staff development programs and staff expectations must include these concepts.

12. Lastly, staff and student organizations must *offer a regular menu of information, programs, and literature* to educate women (and men) about women's issues. Such programming should focus on topics discussed more fully in earlier chapters, including:

- Awareness of the new scholarship on women and suggestions for incorporating this information into the curriculum
- Moral and ethical issues including abortion or the right to life
- Rape (unknown and acquaintance), personal safety, abuse and incest
- Eating disorders (such as anorexia or bulimia) and related issues of body image leading to greater self-acceptance
- Affirmative action including student employment practices
- Sexual harassment, both as it affects students while in college and women once they enter the world of work beyond the campus
- Assertiveness and empowerment in the classroom, in personal relationships, and the world of work—Adrienne Rich (1979) admonishes women students to think of themselves as being in college to *claim* an education, not merely to receive one. "The difference is that between acting and being acted upon, and for women it can literally mean the difference in life and death" (p. 231).
- Leadership and followership issues that go beyond skill

building—raising issues like collaboration and competition, networks and other communication systems, and the concept that the leader of the future is a facilitator (Naisbitt, 1984)

- Raising awareness of women's development by addressing such concepts as affiliation and achievement needs, attribution theory, relationship orientation and connectedness, the role of identity and intimacy, and life stages
- Life planning as a broader concept than career planning, addressing issues of family, leisure, and work
- Health issues like pre-menstrual syndrome, fetal alcohol syndrome, gynecological care, and breast self-exams
- Sexual activity and related issues like birth control, sexually transmitted diseases, sexual activity choices including the choice of celibacy
- Sexual or affectional orientation including three levels of programming: one for lesbian students encouraging their achievement of satisfying lives; another for heterosexual students on understanding and maintaining comfortable relationships with lesbian friends, and in the extreme, raising awareness of homophobic students; and a third level on encouraging healthy heterosexual relationships
- Appreciating women of color, focusing on the different cultural experiences among women along with identifying the bonds that transcend color and committing to combat both overt and covert racism.

Many of these topics present points of controversy that make them difficult issues for our heterogeneous campuses to confront. Topics a student organization can present or a faculty member can approach in the classroom when covered by the protections of academic freedom cannot always be approached by student affairs staff who might not have the same protections. Institutions must make a commitment to grant student affairs staff the same academic freedom of inquiry afforded students and faculty at our institutions. Realistically, however, programs that student affairs staff may not be able to implement because of controversy and political sensitivities can often be offered more effectively by student organizations.

Applying Feminist Models to Student Affairs Divisions

"All feminist politics today is predicated on the belief that women disproportionately occupy peripheral positions in society, that is, roles that are subordinate to, deemed less important than, and accorded lesser rewards than those held by men" (Taylor, 1983, p. 436). Taylor suggests that two major strategies logically follow from this perspective: (1) reform of the system by redistributing people, particularly women, into the core and out of the periphery, or (2) revolution within the system to redistribute rewards by transforming the existing system. Educators must help women see the differences in these strategies. While each may have its place in individual systems, student affairs staff must help student organizations—particularly student government structures—along with our college or university governance and administrative systems to adopt the latter strategy and revolutionize the nature of our systems.

Student affairs professionals must first look to our own structures. Feminist systems are typified as being more egalitarian and collaborative, while the traditional bureaucracy creates many levels of control within the college's hierarchy combined with rigid communication patterns. Whether we call this desired system "feminist" or not, it clearly has a lot of promise for humanizing the world of work. Our student affairs divisions must model the facilitative leadership styles we would like our women and men students to emulate. Student affairs divisions must redesign operations to reduce the barriers between departments. We must work together to share responsibility for students' welfare. We must redesign our structures to create flattened hierarchies and open communication patterns. We must offer women staff all the protections, sensitivities, and development we offer students. A student affairs division that does not recognize nor practice these principles is unlikely to coordinate the institutional revolution needed or offer an appropriate depth of program for women students.

Future Directions for Research

Ongoing research is important to successful programs designed to facilitate the development of women. Research helps to establish facts around which to build programs, target programming goals, and identify factors over which programmers and policy makers have some control (Tangri and Strasburg, 1979). While scholarship on women has increased dramatically over the past decade, we are still just beginning to understand the complexity and variety inherent in the lives of women as well as the variables that are important in their development while in college and across the life span. Three types of research deserve the attention of individuals working with women in college: studies of women's development, evaluation of programs for women, and investigation of the impact of college on women.

Scholars are at last recognizing that women's lives differ in important ways from those of men and deserve to be studied in their own right. We need to continue to investigate both the issues that are important to women across the life span and the ways in which women approach the cognitive and affective dimensions of their lives. Giele (1982) advocates longitudinal, cross-cultural, and naturalistic studies to achieve these goals.

Longitudinal research is particularly important if we are to determine the relative importance of specific issues across the life span and separate historical influences from developmental change. Tracing the lives of specific groups of women over an extended period of time will give us a better picture of the emphasis women place on career, family, and other factors in their lives; the interconnectedness of these dimensions; and the ways in which they handle conflicts and role strain as they age. Particularly important and interesting information can be gathered concerning changes in self-concept, cognitive reasoning, and affective reactions to life events across the life span. Longitudinal study of the lives of women representing different age cohorts is necessary to sort out the effects of changing societal expectations and norms on women's attitudes, decisions, and life experiences. Such studies are especially important in determining changes in development that are internal and that all women can expect to experience at certain points in their lives, and those that are precipitated by external events such as economic conditions or sex-role attitudes. Cross-cultural studies would also help to determine universal developmental variables. Factors that are found to be important in the lives of women regardless of cultural background can more safely be considered characteristic of women's internal development than those characteristic only of a specific sub-population.

Differences among women must also be recognized. Researchers have a tendency to group all women together and assume that their experiences and attitudes are similar. This type of approach fails to give an accurate picture of the diversity that exists in women's lives. We need to investigate the development and life experiences of various sub-groups of women including racial and cultural minorities, lesbians, women of varied socioeconomic backgrounds, and women who choose different life-styles.

Naturalistic studies provide a depth and richness that cannot be obtained from surveys and that are particularly important in the early exploratory stages of any research program. Open-ended interviews and observational techniques often result in information that the researcher would not think to ask for in a survey and that provides direction for future, more focused, research activity. The issues women talk about spontaneously, the affect and meaning they attach to particular events, and their actual behavior in specific situations often provide a clearer picture of women's lives than responses to a questionnaire based on the preconceived ideas of an investigator.

Earlier chapters in this sourcebook have advocated a variety of programs to enhance the development of women. We must do a better job of assessing the effects of specific programs on women. Too often evaluation consists of asking participants if they liked a program rather than determining if it had a positive influence on their attitudes, decision making, or behavior. Evaluation procedures consisting of pre-post measures and follow-up techniques are needed to determine the specific effects of programs. Ongoing observation of programs and periodic monitoring of participants' reactions to programs in progress are also desirable. This type of process evaluation is particularly helpful in ensuring that the program goals and activities are being carried out as intended. It provides an opportunity to modify program components that are not working and to identify particularly helpful aspects of a program.

We must also explore the impact of college on women in a more general way. A number of questions should be addressed.

- Does college differentially impact specific subgroups of women, such as traditional eighteen-to-twenty-two-year-olds, older women returning to college, racial and cultural minorities, lesbians, or first-generation college women?
- What effect does choice of college major have on women? For instance, does a woman majoring in a nontraditional field (such as math, physics, or accounting) face more prejudice, harassment, or barriers than a woman majoring in a traditional field such as humanities or education?
- Does the type and size of institution attended affect women's educational experiences and development?
- Do women who attend college view their lives differently than those who do not go on to college?
- In what ways, if any, does college attendance affect women's life-style decisions, values, and self-concept?
- What factors, if any, within the college environment affect the cognitive development, sex-role orientation, achievement motivation, and affiliation needs of women?

For too long we have assumed that the college experience was uniformly beneficial for all students. We are now beginning to recognize the simplicity and naiveté of this assumption. As educators we have a responsibility to identify and verify our statements. Attending to the outlined research agenda is a challenging yet necessary start in determining how women are affected by their experiences in college. If we are to provide a truly developmental environment, such efforts are imperative.

References

Bean, J. P., and Bradley, R. K. "Untangling the Satisfaction-Performance Relationship for College Students." Paper presented at the annual meeting of the American Educational Research Association, New Orleans, April 26, 1984.

Bernard, J. "Women's Educational Needs." In A. W. Chickering and Associates (Eds.), *The Modern American College: Responding to the New Realities of Diverse Students and a Changing Society.* San Francisco: Jossey-Bass, 1981.

Bolton, C. D., and Kammeyer, K. C. W. *The University Student: A Study of Student Behavior and Values.* New Haven: College and University Press, 1967.

Follett, C. V., Andberg, W. L., and Hendel, D. D. "Perceptions of the College Environment by Women and Men Students." *Journal of College Student Personnel,* 1982, *23* (6), 525–531.

Giele, J. Z. "Future Research and Policy Questions." In J. Z. Giele (Ed.), *Women in the Middle Years.* New York: Wiley, 1982.

Herman, D. "Does Equality Mean Sameness?" In D. L. Fowlkes and C. S. McClure (Eds.), *Feminist Visions: Toward a Transformation of the Liberal Arts Curriculum.* University: The University of Alabama Press, 1984.

Hurst, J. C. "Chickering's Vectors of Development and Student Affairs Programming." In C. A. Parker (Ed.), *Encouraging Development in College Students.* Minneapolis: University of Minnesota Press, 1978.

Johnson, S. *Survey of Institutional Adaptations.* Berkeley, Calif.: Carnegie Council on Policy Studies in Higher Education, 1979.

Levine, A. *When Dreams and Heroes Died: A Portrait of Today's College Students.* San Francisco: Jossey-Bass, 1980.

Minnich, E. K. "From Fate to Inheritance." In E. M. Bender, B. Burk, and N. Walker (Eds.), *All of Us Are Present.* Columbia, Mo.: James Madison Wood Research Institute, 1984.

Naisbitt, J. *Megatrends.* New York: Warner Books, 1984.

Rich, A. *On Lies, Secrets, and Silence.* New York: Norton, 1979.

Tangri, S. S., and Strasburg, G. L. "Where Research and Policy Connect: The American Scene." In V. Lipman-Blumen and J. Bernard (Eds.), *Sex Roles and Social Pollicy.* Beverly Hills, Calif.: Sage, 1979.

Taylor, V. "The Future of Feminism in the 1980s: A Social Movement Analysis." In L. Richardson and V. Taylor (Eds.), *Feminist Frontiers: Rethinking Sex, Gender, and Society.* Reading, Mass.: Addison-Wesley, 1983.

Susan R. Komives is dean of student life at Stephens College. She is a former president of the American College Personnel Association.

Nancy J. Evans is assistant professor of higher education and student affairs at Indiana University. She has held positions in residence life, student activities, and counseling at several colleges and universities.

Persons interested in the development of women can consult recent literature exploring women's concerns and intervention strategies.

Sources of Additional Information

Cathleen M. Barrett
Nancy J. Evans

During the last decade, women's development has received significant attention from scholars and researchers. Although we know more about women than previously, we must remember that the new scholarship on women is still in its infancy. Studies are generally exploratory and suggestions for developmental interventions are often unevaluated. In spite of these limitations, student affairs practitioners will find a growing body of helpful literature to augment their knowledge of issues facing women as they develop across the life span. This chapter presents a representative selection of readily available books and articles related to women's development and programming.

General Readings

Adelstein, D., Sedlacek, W. E., and Martinez, A. "Dimensions Underlying the Characteristics and Needs of Returning Women Students." *The Journal of the National Association for Women Deans, Administrators, and Counselors,* 1983, *46* (4), 32–37.
    The purpose of this article was to identify the population of returning women students as a heterogeneous group whose specific

N. J. Evans (Ed.). *Facilitating the Development of Women.* New Directions for Student Services, no. 29. San Francisco: Jossey-Bass, March 1985.

needs are defined by a variety of life circumstances. Emphasis was placed on the importance of programs that are designed to target subgroups of women based on current life circumstances.

Baruch, G., Barnett, R., and Rivers, C. *Life Prints: New Patterns of Love and Work for Today's Women.* New York: McGraw-Hill, 1983.
Written for general readership, this book is based on a study conducted in 1979–1980 involving 300 women between the ages of thirty-five and fifty-five. Women representing six different family and employment combinations were included. Well-being was found to be related to two dimensions: mastery and pleasure. Factors influencing these variables are discussed.

Cox, S. *Female Psychology: The Emerging Self.* Chicago: Science Research Associates, 1976.
This compilation of articles provides an overview of the psychological well-being of women in relation to sexuality, nonconscious self-statements, learned helplessness, minority women's issues, and the power of modeling. Traditional assumptions about women and happiness are analyzed.

Giele, J. Z. (Ed.). *Women in the Middle Years.* New York: Wiley, 1982.
This book, a collection of essays evolving from a year-long seminar series organized by the editor, presents information concerning the development and life experiences of middle-aged women. Chapters present a review and analysis of research concerning women's health, the relational orientation of women, women's work and family roles, and the effects of cultural factors and social policy on women. An agenda for research and social policy is proposed. Data bases relevant to women's development are also listed and discussed in an appendix.

Gilligan, C. *In a Different Voice: Psychological Theory and Women's Development.* Cambridge, Mass.: Harvard University Press, 1982.
This book, a summary of some of Gilligan's earlier work, identifies weaknesses in traditional psychological theory with regard to the moral development of women. The chapters address issues of self in relation to others, change, cognition and judgment, and maturity. Gilligan's work offers new ways of organizing one's thinking about women and their development.

Goodstein, L. D., and Sargent, A. G. "Psychological Theories of Sex Differences." In A. G. Sargent (Ed.), *Beyond Sex Roles.* St. Paul, Minn.: West Publishing, 1977.

The authors examine nonbiological theories of sex difference including Freudian psychoanalytic, social learning, and cognitive theories of sex typing. These perspectives are discussed as a framework for understanding how women and men have come to view themselves stereotypically.

Lowenthal, M. F., Thurner, M., and Chiriboga, D., and Associates. *Four Stages of Life: A Comparative Study of Women and Men Facing Transitions.* San Francisco: Jossey-Bass, 1975.

This book presents the results of one of the few major studies of adult development exploring the lives of both men and women. Four pretransitional groups are included in the sample: high school seniors, young newlyweds, middle-aged parents approaching the "empty nest" stage, and older individuals close to retirement. Intensive interviews as well as several structured instruments were used to explore family life, patterns of friendship, self-concept, well-being, sources of and adaptation to stress, and values. Significant sex differences are reported.

McGuigan, D. G. (Ed.). *Women's Lives: New Theory, Research, and Policy.* Ann Arbor: University of Michigan, Center for Continuing Education of Women, 1980.

This book includes a collection of papers presented at a symposium at the University of Michigan addressing issues in the lives of women. Recent research findings in the areas of career involvement, family roles, achievement orientation, health, and other aspects of women's development are presented.

Sargent, A. G. "Minority Women's Issues." In A. G. Sargent (Ed.), *Beyond Sex Roles.* St. Paul, Minn.: West Publishing, 1977.

Although statistically outdated, this article serves as an introduction for two others in the same book on black and Chicano women. Sargent describes the plight of minority women as one of double discrimination, encompassing both sexism and racism.

Examples of Programming

Bauer, B. G. "Bulimia: A Review of a Group Treatment Program." *Journal of College Student Personnel,* 1984, *25* (3), 221–227.

The symptoms and causes of bulimia are reviewed as an introduction to discussion of a group treatment approach found to be successful in working with students experiencing this disorder. The article presents issues that arise in counseling bulimics as well as counseling interventions.

Buckner, D. R. "Developing Coed Residence Hall Programs for Sex-Role Exploration." *Journal of College Student Personnel*, 1981, *22* (1), 52–59.

Buckner discusses the importance of addressing sex-role stereotypes during the college years and suggests that a coed residence hall environment provides an excellent setting in which to explore this issue. A required class on sociology of sex roles for residents of a coed floor is suggested as one programming alternative.

Gelwick, B. P. (Ed.). *Up the Ladder: Women Professionals and Clients in College Student Personnel.* Cincinnati: American College Personnel Association, 1979.

Part two of this monograph presents practical suggestions for the organization and implementation of women's programming. The special needs of minority women, returning women students, and women attending community and junior colleges are discussed. Special attention is devoted to career development programs for women.

Hanson, L. S., and Rapoza, R. S. (Eds.). *Career Development and Counseling of Women.* Springfield, Ill.: Thomas, 1978.

Although rather dated, the research findings and essays included in this volume present an excellent introduction to the factors involved in the career decisions of women. Counseling approaches and issues related to career development are also reviewed.

McGraw, L. K. "A Selective Review of Programs and Counseling Interventions for the Re-entry Woman." *Personnel and Guidance Journal*, 1982, *60* (8), 469–472.

This article discusses programs designed to assist re-entry women in adjusting to college and successfully completing their degrees. Counseling issues and interventions for this population are also presented.

Obelton, N. B. "Career Counseling Black Women in a Predominantly White Coeducational University." *Personnel and Guidance Journal*, 1984, *62* (6), 365–368.

The importance of the mentor/role-model on the life/career development of black women is emphasized in this article. Obelton describes a workshop model as an alternative to individual career guidance. The workshop format includes opportunities for an in-depth look at specific careers as well as personal interaction with the mentors/models.

Pomrenke, V. E., Dambrot, F. H., and Hazard, B. J. "A Low-Budget Leadership Program for University Women: No Funds Are No Excuse." *Journal of the National Association for Women Deans, Administrators, and Counselors,* 1983, *46* (3), 28–33.

A leadership program offered by faculty and staff cosponsored by a local branch of American Association of University Women is described. The program focused on awareness of traditional and nontraditional sex roles and skills needed by undergraduate women who aspire to and are involved in leadership positions.

Simon, L. A. K., and Forrest, L. "Implementing a Sexual Harassment Program at a Large University." *Journal of the National Association for Women Deans, Administrators, and Counselors,* 1983, *46* (2), 23–29.

The authors describe a comprehensive program that addresses the issue of sexual harassment at a large university. Conditions necessary for implementing such a program, a description of the program itself, and a discussion of the issues raised by the program are discussed.

Sophie, J. "Counseling Lesbians." *Personnel and Guidance Journal,* 1982, *60* (6), 341–345.

This article reviews research exploring lesbian identity issues and life-style and discusses the process of forming a lesbian self-identity. Counseling strategies focusing on the development of social support and acquisition of a positive philosophy are presented.

Taylor, I. C., and McLoughlin, M. B. "Mentoring Freshmen Women." *Journal of the National Association of Women Deans, Administrators, and Counselors,* 1982, *45* (2), 10–15.

A credit course exploring life and career choices for women is discussed in this article. Its main purpose was to broaden the thinking of young college women about academic and career choices. An important component of the course was mentoring provided by faculty women teaching in male-dominated fields.

Weishaar, M., and Sandmeyer, L. "A Model for Short-Term Group Counseling for Women in Nontraditional Majors." *Journal of the National Association for Women Deans, Administrators, and Counselors,* 1983, *47* (1), 31–36.

The authors describe a group counseling approach for women in nontraditional fields. The intervention focuses on the school-to-work transition; assessment of self and the work environment; assertiveness; building support through mentors, models, and networks; multiple role management; and being in the minority.

Cathleen M. Barrett is an assistant professor of counselor education and college student personnel at Western Illinois University, Macomb, Illinois. A graduate of Indiana University, her primary interests are in counselor training and college student development.

Nancy J. Evans is assistant professor of higher education and student affairs at Indiana University. She has held positions in residence life, student activities, and counseling at a number of colleges and universities.

Index

ational barriers for, 66–67; support services for, 68–72
Rich, A., 50, 58, 92, 98, 103
Rivers, C., 106
Robertson, J. F., 19, 26
Rod and Frame Test (FRT), 37–38
Rodgers-Rose, L. F., 75–76, 89
Rollins, B., 16, 26
Rosenkrantz, P. S., 8
Rossi, A. S., 12, 13, 14, 15, 19, 26
Rubin, L. B., 13, 15, 26
Ruiz, R. A., 83, 89

S

Sales, E., 13, 19, 26
Sandmeyer, L., 109
Sangiuliano, I., 13, 26
Santiseban, D., 89
Sargent, A. G., 106, 107
Saslaw, R. S., 71, 73
Scarf, M., 13, 19, 26
Schlossberg, N. K., 9, 12, 13, 14, 26
Scholastic Aptitude Test (SAT), 86
Schroeder, H., 36, 43
Scott, N. A., 62, 67, 68, 70, 71, 73
Sedlacek, W. E., 57, 105–106
Self-concept: developmental interventions for, 55; dimension of, 19–20; of young women, 50–51
Serlin, E., 13, 16, 26
Sheldon, E. B., 15, 17, 26
Sherman, J. A., 37, 38, 44
Simon, L. A. K., 55, 58, 109
Smith, P., 82, 84, 89
Smith-Rosenberg, C., 7, 8
Sophie, J., 49, 58, 109
Squire, S., 50, 58
Squires, R. L., 51, 57
Staff: development of, 98–99; for re-entry women, 71
Stephens College, conference at, 92
Stewart, W. R., 13, 26
Strange, C. C., 48, 58
Strasburg, G. L., 100, 103
Strommer, D. W., 11, 16, 26
Student Information Form, 85
Student services: administrative challenges in, 91–103; agenda for, 96–99; background on, 91–93; barriers to, 93–94; and cognitive development, 38–42; developmental interventions

in, 20–23, 53–56; evaluation of, 102; feminist models for, 99–100; goals of, 77; initiatives in, 94–95; for minority women, 85–88; programming mistakes in, 52–53; readings on, 107–109; for re-entry women, 69–72; research directions for, 100–103; responsibilities of, 56; responsibility for, 95–96
Sue, D. W., 80, 81, 82, 83, 89
Support services: for minority women, 87–88; for re-entry women, 68–72

T

Tamir, L. M., 23
Tangri, S. S., 47, 58, 100, 103
Targ, D., 14, 16, 26
Taylor, I. C., 52, 58, 109
Taylor, V., 99–100, 103
Texas-Austin, University of, faculty attitudes toward adult students at, 66
Thurnher, M., 25, 107
Thurstone, L., 37, 44
Tillich, P., 34, 44
Tittle, C. K., 20, 26, 62, 65–69, 73
Trimble, J. E., 77, 89
True-Homma, R., 81, 90

U

U.S. Bureau of the Census, 62
U.S. Department of Education, 86, 90

V

Vaillant, G. E., 14, 26
Van Dusen, R. A., 15, 17, 26
Ventura, L. A., 49, 57
Vogel, S. R., 8

W

Waite, L. J., 11, 25, 26
Weingarten, K., 14, 24
Weishaar, M., 109
Weissman, M. M., 20, 26
Wells, T., 12, 26
Whiteman, H., 76, 90
Wiersma, J., 14, 26
Wikler, N., 16, 24
Willemsen, E. W., 18, 26